Dwelling in the Wilderness

MODERN MONKS
IN THE AMERICAN WEST

Jason M. Brown

Trinity University Press | *San Antonio*

Trinity University Press
San Antonio, Texas 78212

Cover design by Rebecca Lown
Book design by BookMatters, Berkeley
Cover art: Jason M. Brown

ISBN 978-1-59534-979-8 paper
ISBN 978-1-59534-980-4 ebook

Trinity University Press strives to produce its books using methods
and materials in an environmentally sensitive manner. We favor
working with manufacturers that practice sustainable management of
all natural resources, produce paper using recycled stock, and manage
forests with the best possible practices for people, biodiversity, and
sustainability. The press is a member of the Green Press Initiative, a
nonprofit program dedicated to supporting publishers in their efforts
to reduce their impacts on endangered forests, climate change, and
forest-dependent communities.

The paper used in this publication meets the minimum requirements
of the American National Standard for Information Sciences—
Permanence of Paper for Printed Library Materials, ansi 39.48–1992.

CIP data on file at the Library of Congress

28 27 26 25 24 | 5 4 3 2 1

Printed in Canada

CONTENTS

Introduction

To dwell means to belong to a given place.
CHRISTIAN NORBERG-SCHULZ

After a short presentation on the history of the whitewashed twelfth-century Romanesque chapel, and a few samples of the monastery's homemade liqueurs, I wandered away from the cloister and into a grove of trees. Founded in eleventh-century France, the Carthusian Order is perhaps the most austere of the Roman Catholic monastic orders. The monks live more like solitary hermits than the community-oriented Benedictine and Trappist orders of classical medieval Europe. They are widely respected for their dedication to contemplative prayer.

The year was 2011, and I was in the last few months of joint master's degrees in forestry and theology at Yale University. Our European forestry field trip had stopped at the medieval Carthusian monastery nestled in the rolling hills of rural Slovenia, mostly for the liqueurs, but there was also a small medieval village museum, and several state foresters were there to answer our questions about the management of the surrounding forestland.

After the field trip I would head back to Connecticut for a few more months to join the student-led forest crew in the northeast corner of the state, where I would spend the summer managing the school's extensive forestlands. I was feeling weary from the pace of our travel, sick of the almost daily dose of some version of schnitzel for lunch, and trying to ignore a gnawing anxiety about looming student loan debt and uncertain job prospects. I was also nursing the dull throb of a drawn-out crisis of faith that left my relationship with the Mormon (LDS) faith anything but clear.

I continued walking along an ancient stuccoed wall clothed in a bramble of red roses. The air was humid, and there was a faint

1

Roses press against the wall of a twelfth-century Carthusian monastery

smell of humus and grass in the air. Breaking from my path along
the ancient wall, I wandered a short way into the forest. I stopped
and stood in silence. The forest held the cloister in a soft, vegetative
embrace. I craned my neck to gaze up into the leafy branches of a
cruciform ash tree with veins of liana slithering up a slender bole. As
the sun-dappled leaves flitted and started, my body began to relax
for the first time in a long time, and a sense of calm came over me
like a sudden waft from a cool breeze. There was something about
this place; something unique about the woven threads of land, work,
and prayer that make a monastery utterly fascinated me, and my
mind began to turn with questions.

༄ ༀ

With origins in the ancient desert wilderness of the Levant, Christian monasticism grew from seeds planted by the so-called Desert
Fathers and Mothers, a motley crew of hermits and radical ascetics that twentieth-century monk and writer Thomas Merton

(1915–1968) called "spiritual anarchists."[1] Whereas Roman Catholic friars and priests take the familiar religious vows of poverty, chastity, and obedience to a superior, monks make a vow of stability. From the Latin *stabilitas*, this means they vow to live a life committed to a community and to a place. The cell (a monk's room), the monastery's chapel and refectory, the paths, fields, rivers, hills, and forests become the country monks set out from on a journey seeking union with God. Rooted in place, the seasons, cycles, and biotic community of the monastic landscape become beloved companions on this journey.

What began as an obscure desert movement spread throughout the world. As part of their stability, monasteries have been managing land as both a material and spiritual resource for centuries. Among the Carthusians, the land supports the monks' life of prayer with the proceeds from its agricultural produce and liqueur business. The forests surrounding the monastery serve not only as a physical buffer zone against the noise and concerns of the outside world but also as a spiritual ecology that knits together the inscape of the soul with the surrounding landscape.

Standing in that grove of trees set me on my own amazing journey, one that would lead me into a doctoral program and eventually to four monastic communities in the American West. Along the way, I also learned some valuable lessons about the power of place and how cultivating a deeper sense of place might be an important skill in our troubled and troubling times. But first, a bit more about me.

~ : ~

I was raised in Yorba Linda, a wealthy equestrian suburb that abuts the scrubby Chino Hill State Park in Orange County, California. The Tongva, Chumash, Acjachemen, and Payómkawichum peoples have lived on the idyllic shores of Southern California from time immemorial. Spanish missions, ranchos, and later Anglo-American farmers devastated these peoples. After World War II, houses and strip malls burst from the soil like so many pastel toadstools, and the prosperity gospel was preached in many of the bustling evangelical churches. In its early years marketed as an agriculturalist's Eden and later as a bedroom community to Los Angeles, Orange County is now something of a poster child for the glamorous conspicuous consumption to which many Americans aspire.

When I was about six years old, my parents became active in the Mormon Church or, as they prefer to be called, the Church of Jesus Christ of Latter-day Saints. This became the roots of my own religious life until a mild rebellious phase during my teenage years, when Kurt Cobain and all things grunge became my pseudoreligion.

I settled down, however, and after spending two years as a missionary in the Dominican Republic, I enrolled in an anthropology program at Brigham Young University in Provo, Utah. The campus is nestled between the Wasatch Mountains and the vast freshwater Utah Lake. I was excited to be among so many people of my own faith, and expected to get married and start a family.

This would not be how things worked out, however, and soon my faith in Mormonism began to stagnate. The political climate of Utah and a deep longing for a richer spiritual life left me feeling isolated from my chipper peers. I carried this weight into my master's work in forestry and theology at Yale. Busy as I was, I still felt a nagging existential loneliness and a deep sense of uncertainty about my place in the world.

After I graduated from my master's programs, I landed a university teaching position in Salt Lake City and summer work as a forester with the U.S. Forest Service—putting both my degrees to work. I stepped away from my Mormon practice and began to meditate, to eagerly visit temples of all sorts, cathedrals, synagogues, and mosques. Teaching courses in religious studies and ethics at the university, I, too, became a student of the world's beautiful faiths, especially their common contemplative wisdom, which emphasizes silence, solitude, and, in some cases, the natural world.

It was during this time that I discovered the writings of Thomas Merton, who had almost single-handedly revitalized Catholic contemplative spirituality in the 1950s and 1960s and was enjoying a surge in popularity among spiritual seekers from a variety of backgrounds. I soon learned that Merton's order, the Trappists, had a monastery in Huntsville, Utah, so I decided to go on my first ever monastic retreat.

Perched in a mountain valley of neatly quilted hay and pasture, overlooking impossibly beautiful mountains, the monastery radiated the kind of peace I had been craving for so long. There was a deep power to the place I could not name, but it reminded me of the peace I had felt standing in the monastery forest in Slovenia.

∾ ⁚ ∾

It turned out that being a professional forester for the federal government wasn't for me, so, encouraged by my success as a university lecturer, I decided to go back to school and get my doctorate in the emerging interdisciplinary field of ecological humanities.[2]

On the day I arrived in Vancouver, British Columbia, at the end of July 2013, the air was humid and thick with the smell of decaying mushrooms. It was my first semester of doctoral work, and I had decided to live in Green College, a small, communal dormitory on campus for graduate students.

I pulled into a small parking lot at the University of British Columbia, which is perched on the edge of the continental mainland, and checked in at the residence office. I was told that my dorm was not quite ready, so I decided to explore.

As I descended a steep staircase, step by step the heat and humidity eased, and the sparkle of the Salish Sea began to glimmer through the emerald-green canopy of Douglas fir and big-leaf maple trees that clung to the sandy cliffs. My legs, stiff from the long drive, began to tremble slightly from the repetitive movement. When my feet finally hit sand, I looked up and the shady green of the forest had transformed into tan beach and calmly lapping blue sea. Beyond that, wild rocky shores and distant mountainsides of verdant evergreen forests. I felt as though I had found the long-lost Garden of Eden in the wilds of the Pacific Northwest.

I felt at home in Vancouver's lush coastal rainforest, and soon I found my spiritual home as well. I began attending traditional

Anglican and Catholic services and a contemplative prayer group. Contemplative Christianity became that much-yearned-for well of spiritual sustenance for me.

Finishing my coursework requirements, I began searching for a dissertation topic that would allow me to explore the relationship between religion, spirituality, and ecology. It wasn't long before I remembered my experience at the Carthusian monastery in Slovenia, and the relationship between monks and their landscapes seemed like a perfect project. The power of monastic sacred places, which had led me to Contemplative Christianity, was also a lens through which I could ask questions about the power of place in a world brimming with ecological change and distress.

Over the last several years of fieldwork, writing my dissertation, and now teaching, the reality of anthropogenic climate change has become all too clear. During my first winter in Vancouver, there was hardly any rain at all, and I wondered what all the fuss was about so-called "Rain-couver." The next winter saw a polar vortex that left my neighborhood as icy as the local hockey rink for almost two weeks. Old-growth forests continue to shrink in the province, and more and more rain-loving western red cedar trees are dying out from prolonged heat. Summers are also increasingly blanketed in thick wildfire smoke, and in 2021 we suffered record-breaking temperatures from a heat dome that caused the wildfires that destroyed much of the town of Lytton, British Columbia. I began to realize all too well that ecological crises were not just some abstract concepts out there in the distant future. Climate change is now part of the everyday reality in the place I call home, and for many coastal, northern, and island peoples, climate change will almost certainly be an existential threat within a generation.

～ ： ～

There were only a few days left in my stay at Our Lady of Guadalupe Abbey, nestled in the mossy hills of western Oregon. At approximately 4:13 a.m., just as I had done for the last month, I stumbled in the darkness from my cell toward my creaky choir stall. Just before I reached my seat, I looked up and past the church tabernacle, through the dark west-facing abbey window. The cycle of May's full moon had serendipitously placed her subdued light in glorious view through a light haze, casting her pale glow over the monastery's extensive wooded property.

I recalled that I had arrived under the previous full moon, and though it was a coincidence of my arrival, my stay had spanned an entire lunar month. I had never measured time using this most ancient of clocks, nor had I punctuated days of manual work, silent prayer, and walks in the forest with the communal chanting of the biblical Psalms. But this is life for the monks who call Our Lady of Guadalupe Abbey—and the hundreds of other Christian monastic communities all over the world—home.

What compelled me to participate in this monthlong retreat were questions about the rich relationship monks forge with their places, questions that had first occurred to me in Slovenia, ripened through my eventual conversion to Catholicism, and crafted into a research project during the first year of doctoral work. In committing to live at the monastery for a month, I was seeking the abbot's blessing to return as a researcher, but to do that I had to prove that I could endure the rigors of monastic life without getting in the way of the monks' single-purposed lives. Luckily, by the end of my stay, the abbot was sufficiently persuaded by my monastic countenance, and my hope to become something of a contemplative ethnographer was blessed to move forward!

Academically, I was interested in understanding the phenomenology of place and landscape. This tongue twister of a word simply means the branch of philosophy that seeks to understand our embodied experiences. What interested me as an interdisciplinary scholar of ecological humanities was to understand how monks dwell in their landscapes. How might a tradition that has been so deeply shaped by the biblical symbolism of wilderness, paradise-gardens, mountains, oceans, and trees see the landscape? And how might the features of the landscape contribute to the meanings that are made within the monks' unique sense of place?

So, what is the relationship between places and the wider landscape? With origins in seventeenth-century Dutch painting, *Land-
scap*, equivalent to the German *Landschaft*, means simply the shape
or features of the land (unrelated to how we landscape a front yard).[3]
While its origins stem from landscape painting, it has been taken up
as a useful concept by the social sciences to talk about the ways culture and nature are entangled.

In its broadest sense, landscape includes the totality of the physical, nonhuman features of the world such as geology, soil, atmo-
sphere, and ecosystems. It also includes human settlements, farms,
and protected areas like national parks. It is, in short, both the world
and what we as human beings make of it. It is nature and scenery,
land and ecology, culture and society all woven into a dense fabric.

Place is a specific location with special significance to a person
or group within the landscape. Humans forge deep attachment to
places, so much so that geographer Yi-Fu Tuan enlisted the term
topophilia (*topos* meaning place and *philia* signifying love) to talk
about this relationship.[4] Rootedness and attachment to places are a
basic component of human existence, and *home* is the quintessential
place.[5]

Places, like layers in a geological stratum, accumulate human experiences, affections, histories, identities, and traumas, especially for
communities that span many generations like Indigenous peoples.
Sense of place, as the geographical and environmental psychology
literature suggests, is forged by a long-term, two-way relationship
between people and their landscapes.[6] Monks, it seemed to me, who
put down roots in a single place and vow to live out their lives there
and nowhere else, might have interesting stories to tell about their relationships to place and landscape—relationships that are lush with
an array of spiritual symbols, memories, epiphanies, and experiences.

The Dawn of the Anthropocene

I soon realized, however, that my research had more than just academic implications. We are living through a time of troubling

change, a world that is wracked with the pangs of transition. We are not yet sure if these are the groans of a kind of civilizational death rattle or the guttural sounds of birth. Perhaps they are both. Climate disturbances and warming, pervasive toxic pollution, species extinctions, rapidly advancing permanent deforestation, extreme weather, and drought—each driven by predominantly industrial human-development activities—threaten to radically change the landscapes and seascapes we call home.

The changes are so serious and pervasive that geologists are considering naming the modern era the Anthropocene, the age of humans. Popularized by atmospheric chemist Paul Crutzen in the early 2000s, the Anthropocene is imagined to be the era of peak global human domination.[7] The Anthropocene is not the first attempt to name our increasingly human-heavy era. Catholic priest Antonio Stoppani coined the term *Anthropozoic* in 1873 as a first reference to the human presence on earth with the force of a geological epoch, and French Jesuit priest Pierre Teilhard de Chardin, who imagined the whole cosmos evolving toward God through the human person, coined the term *Noosphere* for the emergence of a global human consciousness that in some ways predicted the internet.[8]

Evidence for the Anthropocene is supported by the fact that humans are now dramatically influencing the planetary carbon, nitrogen, phosphorus, water, and sulfur cycles. Human-produced mercury pollution can be found in ice cores in the Arctic and isolated waterways. Microplastics are pervasive throughout the food web. And though this is somewhat speculative, species extinctions appear to be occurring well above the historical background rates calculated using geological data. This has led scientists to suggest that we are passing through a sixth mass extinction—industrial capitalism now recognized as being equally destructive as toxic gases, snowball earth, volcanic eruptions, and a massive meteor strike.[9]

Climate change, perhaps the greatest threat we face as a species other than widespread nuclear war, is impacting particular places differently. The Arctic region, for example, is warming at a rate that is almost twice, and in some places three or even four times, the global average.[10] Global average surface temperatures have increased by a mean of 0.8 °C over the past 140 years, and the rate is increasing.

As nations gather in global conferences to hammer out timelines for emissions reductions targets that are consistently too little too late, the effects of flooding, drought, blight, and shifting patterns of migration are being felt throughout the world. Business-as-usual projections for the end of the century put average global temperatures somewhere between 2 and 4 °C warming.[11] At the time of this writing, it is increasingly unlikely that we will avoid 2 degrees of warming and its accompanying waves of ecological, climatic changes and massive social disruptions. And as Pope Francis cautions in his 2015 encyclical letter *Laudato si'*, it is the global poor and marginalized who are likely to suffer the brunt of the disasters to come.[12]

For Indigenous peoples of North America, of course, this is all something of an ecologically apocalyptic déjà vu. Indigenous peoples suffered prolonged and sustained invasion, genocide, and marginalization at the hands of settler-colonial imperialism. For peoples who by their own account have been living in their places from time immemorial, whose creation stories often emerged in situ, the globalization of ecocide is all the more troubling.[13]

In the face of this history of ecological mismanagement, exploitation, and destruction, many nature writers, conservationists, and environmental activists have advocated for a recommitment to and deeper love for our places. Conservationist and pioneering wilderness advocate Aldo Leopold (1887–1948), for example, wrote in his seminal *Sand County Almanac* that "we abuse the land because we regard it as a commodity belonging to us. When we see the land as a community to which we belong, we may begin to use it with love and respect."[14] We are more likely to protect and care for a place and its inhabitants if we feel a sense of attachment and love for that place. In other words, while we might need to think globally, we must act, and inevitably live, locally. This sense of belonging to place is something Indigenous peoples all over the world have expressed in various forms for millennia; and it is why colonization is often such a powerful trauma.

Another reason attention to place is increasingly important is that the core strategy of environmentalism, to set aside land in protected and wilderness areas, is being recognized as only one among many strategies within the broader environmental movement. For one thing, climate change does not respect park and wilderness area boundaries. Second, in recent years there has been considerable pushback against nineteenth- and twentieth-century nature writers' view of human beings as separate from the natural world. The *idea* of wilderness as a space without human influence has vanished in a changing climate, but it also risks devaluing the ways people have learned to dwell sustainably in their places over the centuries.

In the Puritan imagination, wilderness was a place that was unknown, unsettled, uncultivated. For example, to Puritan William Bradford (1590–1657), the coast of Massachusetts appeared to be a "hideous and desolate wilderness" compared to his bucolic England, filled with "wild beasts and wild men."[15] This anxiety fueled the frenzied clearing and taming of North America by settler and trader alike.

It wasn't until the works of the Romantic poets like William Wordsworth (1770–1850) or transcendentalists like Ralph Waldo Emerson (1803–1882) and Henry David Thoreau (1817–1862) started to percolate into the collective unconscious that wilderness became the stuff of romance. In Thoreau's essay "Walking," he boldly proclaims that "in wildness is the preservation of the world."[16] Wilderness is constantly calling civilization back to its source. He writes, in stark contrast to the prevalent Christian agrarianism of his day, that "a town is saved, not more by the righteous men in it than by the woods and swamps that surround it."[17] These newly valued wilds took on a deeply spiritual function for the weary urbanite. For Thoreau and many others of his generation, wild places had become sanctuaries of encounter with the divine. "I enter a swamp as a sacred place—a sanctum sanctorum," Thoreau wrote.[18]

In his controversial 1996 essay "The Trouble with Wilderness; or, Getting Back to the Wrong Nature," environmental historian William Cronon shows that the shoots of the wilderness movement

emerged from the roots of Romantic and transcendentalist longing
for the sublime. In this longing, wilderness was understood not as a
space of land needing cultivation but as an original primordial domain that could become a blessed window to the divine, or as divine
itself. Wilderness was also a place to shake off the emasculating
urbanity of Western cities and bask in the glow of one's wild nature.
The national park systems of North America eventually institution-
alized this sense of sacredness that was knit into the national identity, which Ken Burns calls "America's Best Idea."[19]

Cronon argues that this history has resulted in a contemporary
ethos within mainstream environmentalism that elevates wilderness as the gold standard of conservation targets and, by so doing,
tends to leave human beings out of the natural world altogether. He
writes, "Only people whose relation to the land was already alien-
ated could hold up wilderness as a model for human life in nature,
for the romantic ideology of wilderness leaves precisely nowhere for
human beings actually to make their living from the land."[20] Encom-
passing some of our most beautiful and iconic places, wilderness, by
its most common definition, consists of the places where humans do
not dwell. The 1964 U.S. Wilderness Act states that wilderness is a
place "where man [*sic*] himself is a visitor who does not remain." On
a planet that is rapidly approaching ten billion souls, conservation
needs to be more creative about how we propose to live alongside
our more-than-human kin. In other words, in the Anthropocene, we
must learn to better live *with* the land, not just expand the places
where we cannot. As anthropologist Tim Ingold has written, we
need a *dwelling* perspective, meaning one that sees humans as a part
of the landscape, not separate or alien from it, a perspective that has
been integral to Indigenous lifeways for thousands of years in thousands of different ways.[21]

For most urban and modern peoples, however, we have somehow
come to imagine that we are separate from nature and from the land.
Don't believe me? Reflect on this: Do you, generally speaking, perceive yourself as living *on* earth or within or among earth? Going all
the way back to Plato's theory of the Forms as being superior realities

to the things of this world, Christianity inherited this tendency to devalue earthly things for spiritual and heavenly things, so much so that Lynn White Jr. (himself a Presbyterian), in his essay "The Historical Roots of the Ecological Crisis," called the dominant form of modern Christianity the most anthropocentric religious movement the world has ever seen![22] White called Christians to rediscover the legacy of Saint Francis of Assisi, the creature-loving patron saint of ecology. I would, of course, add to this the lifeways of monks as well.

Cronon's call for a revaluation of our homeplaces resonates with and echoes the themes of another Christian writer who is also a farmer, Wendell Berry. Berry took up a short correspondence with Thomas Merton and has been one of the most celebrated contemporary champions of a fierce love and commitment to place, both as a kind of elemental human spiritual necessity and as a tactic in responding to ecological destruction.

Berry began his career as a New York–based novelist, but in 1965 he and his family abruptly decided to buy a small farm in Henry County, Kentucky, where he had been born. Berry's life and writing are critical of wanton ecological destruction, industrial-scale agriculture, and rampant consumerism. Berry spends most of his time on this farm, and interviewers and journalists must be willing to help out if they want to speak with him. As British author Paul Kingsnorth writes in the introduction to his collection of essential writings by the farmer-poet, "Wendell Berry's formula for a good life and a good community is simple and pleasingly unoriginal. Slow down. Pay attention. Do good work. Love your neighbours. Love your place. Stay in your place. Settle for less, enjoy it more."[23] Berry's voluminous poetry and prose reveal a tenderhearted sense of place that is characterized by a slow-cultivated, intimacy-seeking knowledge of the land through work, observation, and contemplation. In an era of rapid change, a strong sense of and love for places could become not only an anchor for coordinating our collective response to multiple crises but also a soothing balm for the human heart in times of trouble.

~ ∶ ~

Enter an unlikely set of heroes. Contemporary Roman Catholic monks put down deep roots and develop unique relationships to their places. Monastic communities, from their earliest moments as spiritual warriors in the desert wilds of Egypt, Judea, and Syria to the thousands of contemporary monastic communities all over the world, have come to see their places as an integral part of their lives of balancing work and contemplative prayer.

The father of Christian monasticism is said to be Saint Anthony the Great of Egypt (251–356 CE). Though he was a harsh ascetic, the desert wilds of the Sinai worked their way into his warrior heart:

> And having journeyed with them [Bedouin traders] three days and
> three nights, he came to a very lofty mountain, and at the foot of
> the mountain ran a clear spring, whose waters were sweet and very
> cold; outside there was a plain and a few uncared-for palm trees....
> Anthony then, as it were, moved by God, *loved the place*, for this was
> the spot which he who had spoken with him by the banks of the
> river had pointed out. So having first received loaves from his fellow
> travelers, he abode in the mountain alone, no one else being with
> him. And recognizing it as his own home, he remained in that place
> for the future.[24]

Saint Anthony loved the place and recognized it as his home. Subsequent generations of monastic communities would adopt this path of staying in one place through the vow of stability.

Twelfth-century Cistercian abbot Stephen Harding (1050–1134) wrote that all good monks should become "lovers of the place" because rootedness was an anchoring point of their journey to God. The paradoxical placelessness of monastic Christian heavenly hope was tethered to and found expression in particular places.

The rich sense of place that monks develop over their lives is imbued with the symbolism of the Bible. The paradise-garden and the desert wilderness are rich spiritual motifs that tint monks' relationship to place and landscape. Unlike the human-excluding wilderness ethic, monks quite literally seek to dwell in the wilderness, often the wild places at the edges of society but also the feral tangle of the wilds of their own souls.

The title of this book plays with what, to contemporary environmentalism, is a paradox. To *dwell in the wilderness* is not only to seek God in the wilderness of the human heart but also, as Cronon and Berry argue, to fall in love with the wildness of the world, especially those places closest to home. Having connected monasticism to sense of place, before I begin the account of my journey with these wilderness-loving monks, I want to say a bit about more about the character of monastic spirituality and situate this work in the modest but growing literature on monastic and contemplative ecology.

A Primer on Monastic Spirituality

The word *monk* comes to us from the Greek root *mono*, meaning one. A *monakos* was a solitary, similar to a *heremos*, or hermit. Throughout its history, the Catholic Church has accommodated a variety of orders and spiritualities related to contemplation and prayer. Each of these religious orders often develops its own unique way of worshipping, its own relationship to the world, and its own form of spirituality. There are Benedictine, Trappist, Franciscan, Dominican, Carmelite, and Jesuit spiritualities, all with their own saints, teachers, writings, values, and practices, all contained within the Catholic fold. Other communions, such as the Oriental and Eastern Orthodox churches or the Anglican churches, also have a range of monastic orders.

The Liturgy of the Hours

Liturgy refers to any public worship service in a religious setting. The organizing activity of any contemporary monastery is the "Liturgy of the Hours" or "Divine Office." This is both a form of worship and a container for monastic spirituality. The Liturgy of the Hours is said to sanctify the hours of the day and to fulfill the psalmist's admonition that "seven times a day I will praise you for your just decrees"

(119:164). The unfolding of the Liturgy of the Hours harmonizes with the physical hours of the day and its seasons. Morning and night, light and dark, stillness and movement, winter and summer— all have rich spiritual resonances across the Northern Hemisphere.

The Psalms, the core of the Liturgy of the Hours, are the ancient Hebrew prayers that, by tradition, are often attributed to King David; however, biblical scholarship is confident that the Book of Psalms has many authors who span over five centuries.[25] It is certain that Jesus of Nazareth prayed the Psalms, and much of his life as a prophet was filtered through the imagery of the psalmists (see, for example, Psalm 22). The genres of the Psalms span the gamut of human emotion and royal court imagery. Many of the Psalms are styled as hymns of praise lavished upon God as a powerful king. Others wail in the mode of communal or individual laments that mourn loss or despair over God's perceived absence. Many more include songs of thanksgiving that invoke God as the merciful protector of the nation of Israel.[26]

The Psalms are also rich with agrarian and pastoral symbolism. The very first psalm, for example, compares the righteous person to a tree:

> Blessed indeed is the man
> who follows not the counsel of the wicked,
> nor stands in the path with sinners . . .
> He is like a tree that is planted beside the flowing waters,
> that yields its fruit in due season,
> and whose leaves shall never fade;
> and all that he does shall prosper.

In addition to extensive references to lament, conquest, and vengeance, the symbolism of the Psalms is often taken from the natural world, invoking the seasons of the year, the cycles of the day, and the elements as well as rivers, mountains, glens, deserts, and valleys. Several even portray the earth praising God as an agent within the poem itself. Psalm 66 begins, "Cry out with joy to God, all the earth; O sing to the glory of his name," and Psalm 96 echoes, "Then will all the trees of the wood shout for joy at the presence of the Lord." These poetic conventions are symbolic yet may capture a Hebrew animistic tendency that was then translated into a monotheistic metaphysics of creation giving praise to its Creator.

Chanting the Psalms is a deeply moving spiritual practice that led monk and writer Thomas Merton to call them "bread in the wilderness," a symbolic allusion to spiritual food in the wilderness of both the traditional setting of the monk and wilds of the soul. For many monks who have chanted them over the years, the language of the Psalms has become second only to breathing. The imagery is a template for understanding the world around them and the world within them, the landscape and the inscape converging in the chanted word.

Eucharist

Embedded in the Liturgy of the Hours is the heart of Catholic worship: the Eucharist. Seen as the "source and summit" of the Catholic faith, the Eucharist is the ritual reenactment of Christ's sacrificial body and blood made present through the earthly elements of bread and wine. From the Greek *Eukharistia*, meaning thanksgiving or gratitude, the Eucharist memorializes the Last Supper before Jesus's death on the cross. Before he died, Jesus was with his disciples in Jerusalem for Passover, in which Jews memorialize their liberation from Egypt by preparing a Passover lamb. In New Testament theology, especially that of the apostle Paul, Jesus himself becomes the paschal sacrifice on behalf of the Christian community that is then memorialized and consumed by the Christian faithful. Most monasteries have half a dozen monks who are ordained priests and therefore will say Mass each day, usually after the Office of Lauds.

The prayers spoken by the priest are said to transubstantiate the bread and wine into Christ's divine body and blood. Though this belief existed in nascent form in the earliest times of the church, the Catholic dogma of transubstantiation was fully fleshed out during the era of scholastic metaphysics (1100–1700 CE). As the priest raises first the bread and then the wine, he repeats the words of Jesus at the Last Supper: "This is my body" and "this is my blood." Catholics do not see this as a symbolic gesture but as a metaphysical, if mysterious, reality. As Catholic novelist Flannery O'Connor is famous for saying of the real presence of Christ in the Eucharist, "If it's just a symbol, to hell with it!"[27] This Eucharistic understanding of the world provides a powerful spiritual connection between the fruits of the land, human labor, and God's grace.

Contemplation

In addition to the Eucharist and the Liturgy of the Hours, monks are also expected to spend time in private prayer. While we often think of prayer as a kind of petition to God that uses poetic words, contemplative prayer, or mental prayer, as it is also known, is much closer to what one might think of as meditation. *Contemplatio* in Latin means to look at or observe, and while some contemplative prayer directs practitioners to focus on specific images such as the passion of Jesus, there is also a strong tradition of contemplative prayer that seeks to grow outward from the sacred words, ideas, metaphors, and concepts of scripture in order to dwell in the raw presence of God, who is believed to be ultimately beyond any of our ideas about God. This "negative" or *apophatic* (from Greek, meaning "other than spoken") prayer complements the "positive" or *cataphatic* ("according to the word" in Greek) prayer that is spoken in the liturgy, scriptures, and sermons.[28] Their combination, the spoken and the unspoken, the known and the unknown, make up two sides of the same contemplative coin and point to a placelessness at the heart of the monastic sense of place.

Lectio Divina

Lastly, monks engage in a daily practice called Lectio Divina. This Latin phrase refers to the contemplative "divine reading" of the Bible. Rather than reading to get through a certain number of passages or chapters during a given time, the monk slowly reads a short passage seeking to uncover its deeper, hidden, or personal meaning. Lectio is traditionally divided into four modes, or steps, though one can jump between them while reading: *lectio, meditatio, oratio,* and *contemplatio* (reading, meditation, prayer, and contemplation). Reading is the straightforward moving through a given passage, while meditation includes taking a deeper look at the passage's characters, symbols, and meanings. Lectio steeps the monks in the language, imagery, and symbolism of the biblical world. Then one can pick out certain phrases or ideas and use them as prayers, lifting the words back up to God. Finally, in contemplation, the words on the page lead one into the deeper well of spiritual silence (apophasis) wherein one encounters God beyond the sacred words and images.[29]

Situating This Book

While *Dwelling in the Wilderness* draws on historical and theological works, it is primarily a firsthand account of the lived experiences of contemporary men's monastic communities (as a man, the men's communities were more accessible to me). The dialogue and quotations come from the transcripts of more than fifty interviews I conducted with monks at four monastic communities in the western states of Oregon, California, and New Mexico. Unlike my dissertation, however, this book is not a theoretical distillation of monastic sense of place but a personal reflection on what the monks I came to know taught me about being more present to the places where I spend time.

Like my academic background in anthropology, forestry, and theology, this work is interdisciplinary. I draw from the fields of theology, nature writing, ethics, and contemporary philosophy. Broadly speaking, this work is part of the burgeoning academic fields of religion and ecology or environmental—or, as I prefer, *ecological*—humanities. Terms such as *spiritual* or *contemplative ecology* are more often enlisted in activist circles.

In recent years there has been a modest increase in books related to monastic and contemplative spirituality, and an even more modest bump in relating that spirituality to what is called contemplative or spiritual ecology. Spiritual or contemplative ecology is a loosely based movement that suggests there is a moral and spiritual root to our ecological problems. Sufi writer Llewellyn Vaughn-Lee suggests that spiritual ecology is a movement that seeks to heal our "image of separateness" from a sacred earth. Technological solutions will be necessary, but as he and others intuit, "the world is not a problem to be solved; it is a living being to which we belong."[30] Sense of place, as I will be discussing it here, has many overlaps with this approach to activism. Though I am not focused on spiritual ecology specifically, my work with sense of place contributes to this literature by adding extensive in-depth conversations with monks themselves, which in my view has been lacking in the literature so far. But to be clear, I am standing on the shoulders of giants.

In *The Cloister Walk* (1996), poet and writer Kathleen Norris reflects on the time she spent among the monks of Saint John's Benedictine Abbey in Collegeville, Minnesota. Her musings run the gamut of contemporary society, spirituality, and monastic history and highlight the perennial wisdom of monasticism's approach to work and prayer. Importantly, she also highlights how powerful the monastic rhythm of day and season can be in calling our awareness to the world around us, and how any of us can adopt this practice without necessarily needing to join a monastery.[31]

The writings of Presbyterian theologian Belden Lane explore the relationship between place and the sacred, particularly among American Christians. His astute observations range from Puritan nature spirituality to contemporary wilderness hiking. His writings have nourished a budding spiritual ecology and ecological theology, and they have been a constant companion in my own writing. His book *The Solace of Fierce Landscapes* (1998) weaves reflections about desert and mountain spirituality together with the grief and agony of accompanying his mother through her slow death from cancer. His book is not only a rich source on monastic wisdom and the spirituality of wilderness and place; it is also a relatable lament. For Lane, contemplative ecology is the beating heart of the Christian tradition and shares no part of Christendom's bloody entanglements with dualistic world-denial, dominionism, colonialism, and capitalistic greed.

In the encyclopedic *Blue Sapphire of the Mind: Notes for a Contemplative Ecology* (2012), theologian Douglas E. Christie outlines primarily historic and theological monastic approaches to place and ecology. Christie, a scholar of early Christianity, organizes the book around seven traditional monastic values or spiritual practices that he sees as particularly relevant to contemporary ecological awareness. Primary among these are *Prosoche*, the art of attention; *Logos*, a theology of creation that sees the world as expressions, or "words," spoken into being by God; *Topos*, or the relationship to land embodied in the monastic vow of stability and place-based spirituality; and *Telos*, the paradoxical emphasis on living in paradise in the present moment. Christie sees ecological literacy and spiritual depth as complementary, and his book is not only historically illuminating but also a powerful manual for the practice of contemplative place-making.[32]

Most akin to my own contemplative ethnography is the work of Sarah McFarland Taylor, who documents a movement of Green Sisters, vowed Catholic women who have integrated ecological issues into their liturgy, theology, and spiritual practices. Most of these women are not necessarily monastic in the strict sense of the term, but Taylor shows how contemporary Catholic women religious are adapting liturgical and spiritual practices to the writings of contemporary self-described "geologian" Thomas Berry (1914–2009), who advocated for an earthier Christianity.[33] Some have started organic farms, green businesses, or innovative ways of honoring the seasons through ritual. Taylor's book is an excellent scholarly case study in the fields of ecological humanities and religion and ecology.

I hope to illustrate just how richly woven together religious symbol and embodied experience can be in the lives of Catholic monks. By demonstrating the richness of the monastic sense of place, I am not suggesting that we all become monks or Catholics. Rather, I aim to show that by more intentionally opening ourselves to place, we are not only enriching our ecologically entangled lives but preparing ourselves for the struggles ahead.

A Note on the Monks' Identities and Quotations

I have decided to use pseudonyms for the monks referenced in this book. For those monks who have published works, however, especially those cited here, I have used their real names, since citation etiquette dictates I do so anyway. For most of the pseudonyms, I chose, in random order, from the list of characters in Umberto Eco's *Name of the Rose*, a murder mystery set in a sixteenth-century Cluniac monastery. Other names were taken from a list of ancient Irish saints who have a reputation for being close to the land. In keeping with this practice of protecting the monks' anonymity, all of the monks are referred to as brothers even if they have been ordained priests. Some of the monks' quoted words have been smoothed out a bit for flow, meaning, and grammar.

Living on the Edge of the World

NEW CAMALDOLI HERMITAGE

> Monasticism, more than any other movement in the history
> of Christendom, has been associated with wilderness.
>
> SUSAN P. BRATTON

The Pacific Coast Highway in central California stiches a meandering seam between rugged, tan mountains splotched with camouflage
green and the blue infinity of the Pacific Ocean. Nearing the end of
a long drive from Vancouver to just south of Big Sur, each undulating curve seemed to offer more beauty than the last. Approaching
the turnoff that leads to New Camaldoli Hermitage, I began to feel
nervous and plagued by the familiar demon of self-doubt. As a green
doctoral researcher, I was worried that my project was too big. My
mind raced as anxiety perched on my shoulder, whispering questions
into my ear to which I had no answers. Would these silence-loving
monks be willing to talk with me? Were my research questions too
scattered? What if, after I got home, I couldn't make sense of the
interviews and my dissertation languished? Or worse, what if my
supervisors didn't like it and I failed to graduate?

I took a deep breath and tried to brush my fears aside by steal-
ing quick glances out the window at the yawning blue of the Pacific. Finally, the sign for the hermitage appeared, and I turned off
the highway and onto a steep lane that seemed to ascend straight
up into a scrubby mountain. Arriving at the monastery campus, I
pulled into a gravel parking lot and hopped out of my truck on stiff

A view of the Pacific Ocean past the New Camaldoli Hermitage chapel

legs. I stood for a moment in the calm balm of the place and couldn't help but recall the peace I had felt amid the trees of the Carthusian monastery not that many years ago, a peace that has been sought at hermitages and monasteries around the world since at least the third century. Here, perched on the edge of California, the monks of New Camaldoli were imitating a way of life that was almost two thousand years old.

Wilderness places like Big Sur have always attracted those who don't quite fit the mold. In its early decades, Christianity was a subversive sect of Judaism and suffered occasional persecutions at the hands of the usually religiously tolerant Roman authorities for their refusal to venerate the emperor. More and more Romans, many of them former slaves, were drawn to Christianity because of the young church's care for the poor, sick, and elderly. Eventually, with the reign of the Emperor Constantine, Christianity became more mainstream. This is partially because in the year 313, Constantine published the Edict of Milan, which officially legalized Christian worship, bringing it, in some cases literally, out from underground. Then, in the year 380, the Emperor Theodosius I issued the revolutionary Edict of Thessalonica, which made Christianity the official religion of the vast Roman Empire. As the religious clerisy and the civil service were joined, some felt that Christianity was becoming corrupt, worldly, watered down, and decadent.

Ascetics and hermits fled to the wilderness to battle their demons and purify their souls, but also to flee military conscription, marriage, and what they saw as the rife corruption of society. The patron saint of these hermits, and one of the first to live full-time deep in the Egyptian desert, was Saint Anthony the Great of Egypt. After a powerful conversion experience, Anthony sold all his possessions— as Jesus had commanded the rich man to do in the New Testament books of Luke and Matthew—and attached himself to an unnamed spiritual teacher. After mastering his teachings, Anthony moved farther and farther from human settlements, seeking greater silence and solitude—first to a graveyard, then an abandoned Roman barracks, and finally to what would become his famous mountain hermitage in the Egyptian desert.

The physical features of the desert—vast vistas, open skies, naked rock, and sparse vegetation—modeled the deep silence and simplicity Anthony sought. The desert was also a spiritual battlefield upon which he sought a spiritual form of martyrdom.[34] Within several decades of the publication of Athanasius's fourth-century *Life of Anthony*, thousands of seekers, mostly men but also women, flocked to the parched wildlands to try their hand at the spiritual life. They had read about John the Baptist's rugged abode on the Jordan River and Jesus's forty days in the wilderness, and wanted to live a more authentic way of life than the Christianity that was emerging in the cities and towns of the Roman Empire.

As Belden Lane has suggested, the harshness of the desert, on the edge of society, pushed people to their own edges.[35] The desert was a place out of bounds, teasing the boundary between life and death, body and soul, heaven and earth. The desert, with its stark beauty and winnowing danger, incarnated the path the hermit sought to travel in his spiritual life. The desert is then, in anthropological language, a liminal space, a space that is betwixt and between, a place that initiates those who can endure its rigors and deprivations.

In the hagiographical literatures that developed around these desert saints, we read simple teachings of virtue, silence, and sacrifice. Included in these accounts is the deep rapport these hermits gained with the desert wilderness itself. In addition to the story of Anthony, who came to love his place in the scorching desert, there are many stories of monks developing friendships with wild animals, even large predators such as hyenas and lions. It is told that the Egyptian hermit Theon would often go on long walks in the desert at night in the company of wild beasts. It is rumored that Paul the Hermit was so beloved by a pair of lions that when he died they were deeply saddened and dug his grave. Macarius of Alexandria was said to have healed a blind hyena pup. And Abba Gerasimus dressed a wounded lion's paw, after which the lion refused to leave his company.[36] The affinity of these monks with the deserts and wild animals was understood not just as an eccentricity but as a sign that in their hearts they had reclaimed something of their longed-for home in the paradise-garden of Eden, and it was beginning to break through into the world around them.

∾ ∶ ∾

Standing just about anywhere at New Camaldoli Hermitage, one is mesmerized by the emerald blue of the ocean and the ever-changing vault of the Pacific sky. A deep stillness enveloped the place like a fog as I made my way to the small reception-area bookstore and entered through a rickety screen door. I was greeted by a middle-aged monk who beamed with kindness. He was dressed in the Camaldolese's distinctly white cassock. After shaking my hand and introducing himself, he phoned the prior to inform him that I had arrived. We exchanged a few pleasantries, and he asked about my journey while we waited.

He soon returned to his tasks, and as I thumbed through a thin volume written by one of the monks, the prior entered the bookstore with a burst of purposeful energy. He was a slender and fit man who was somehow both calm and energetic at the same time. He greeted me with a firm handshake and a smile, and we were off. He walked briskly toward my soon-to-be hermitage, which was walled off by a brick fence and a wooden gate. The gate was arched and had a small cross cut into the wood. Below the cross was a plaque with the name of St. John the Baptist carved into it.

New Camaldoli Hermitage, originally named Immaculate Heart Hermitage, was founded in 1958 by fourteen monks from the ancient Camaldoli Hermitage located in the Casentinesi mountains of Italy, within what is today one of the largest national parks in the country. New Camaldoli spans some 880 acres of coastal wilderness along the Santa Lucia mountain range just southwest of Cone Peak, the second highest peak in the range at 5,155 feet. The Camaldoli monks were drawn to the Big Sur coast for its remoteness, quiet, and beauty. Prior to the purchase of the property by the Camaldolese Order, the property was run as a guest ranch.

Leading me through the gate, the prior began talking about the liturgical schedule—where I needed be at what time. I listened anxiously to my newfound duties as an observer-monk. Opening the unlocked door to my guest hermitage, the prior stood to one side and pointed as he named each simple feature of my new home: chair, bed, bookshelf, and a small bathroom. The place felt cozy, if austere. The prior then excused himself on business to allow me to get settled. He gave me a print version of the schedule and said he hoped to see me at the chanted Office of Vespers at 5:00 p.m. sharp, unless perhaps I was too tired from the drive.

I assured the prior I would be there and closed the door. I unpacked my simple effects and marveled that all the planning, emailing, and proposal writing had finally come to life. I smiled a bit with excitement at the task ahead of me but also cringed a little at the familiar tug of nervousness and anxiety. I had a few hours before the Office of Vespers, so I left the rest of the unpacking for later and decided to explore.

About twenty-five cinder block monastic hermitages cluster around the central chapel. Cooking and laundry facilities, a library,

several staff residences, workshops, and toolsheds spread along
a loose north–south axis up toward the road that climbs into the
mountains. Many of the workspaces were adorned with dusty stat-
ues of saints, crucifixes, or fading icons of Mary, sanctifying even the
most quotidian of tasks, from laundry to recycling.

The large cinder block chapel that centers the campus is topped
with an octagonal dome and flanked by an unadorned bell tower.
All the buildings had a sort of 1970s modern design that I admit
was not immediately appealing to me. Some felt more like strip mall
dentist offices or apartment buildings than contemplative monastic
spaces, but they soon grew on me as I settled into the rhythm of
monastic life.

The hermitage only holds three offices from the Liturgy of the
Hours publicly and daily Mass. This was fewer than other monastic
communities, which is a characteristic of the Camaldolese vocation
and their emphasis on solitude and contemplative prayer. The hermitage's main source of income is hospitality, hosting retreatants.
In the 1970s the monks also opened a small fruitcake bakery that
recently added a (delicious) line of granola. In the 1980s they also
opened a spiritual bookstore that sells local art, jewelry, and many
popular titles by spiritual and religious writers of many faiths. Several of the monks themselves have art, music, and books on the
shelves.

∼: ∼

From my hermitage, I made my way past the chapel through the
cloister garden as the fountain gurgled in the California sun. I
breathed in the warm, ocean-heavy air in deep drafts to unwind
the fatigue of my winding drive. The uncloistered cloister garden
was lush with fruit trees, opulent flowers, and the tangerine flower-
spears of birds of paradise. I sat for a while by the fountain and took
in the sierra outline of coastal peaks.

After ten minutes or so, feeling more present to body and place,
I decided to walk past the refectory and library along the dirt road
that leads into the mountains. Songbirds were flitting through the

garden trees, and turkey vultures lazily coasted on the updrafting air. The steep canyons are Mediterranean in climate, and the evergreen crowns of coastal live oak grow in twisted clusters of army green. The cool canyons shelter some of the southernmost reaches of the coast redwood. Gray fox, mountain lion, black bear, coyote, rattlesnakes, mule deer, birds of prey such as the red-tailed hawk, and a recovering colony of California condors also make their homes with the monks.

The area is located along the San Andreas Fault, and earthquakes are common. The steep slopes are quite erodible, and heavy rains frequently cause mudslides. Highway 1 has even been closed on several occasions, cutting off the monks from their already tenuous link to the outside world. The chaparral hillsides are also very flammable, and major fires have occurred in 1977, 1985, 1999, 2008, and again in 2016, with the monks being evacuated in 1985 and 2008. Father Robert Hale (1937–2018), a monk and former prior of the community, joked in his memoir that they are "living in the shake and bake eschatological adventures of earthquakes and fire."[37]

Walking along the dusty road that extends behind the hermitage, I could see just how flammable the landscape really is. The oak and brush form thickets, and leaf litter forms a crackling carpet of tinder. Staff cabins, a dilapidated barn, sheds, and an old incinerator lined the road. There was also a large diesel generator that chugged and smoked as I passed. The community relies on the generator for electricity, but many of the monks hope to eventually replace it with a solar panel array. I walked past what looked like an overgrown olive orchard, choked with brush and dried grass. As I would learn, they were indeed olive trees and had been planted by the founders from Italy. The enterprise had been abandoned, however, as the monks became more American and failed to keep it up, but the grove stands as a physical reminder of the founding generation of monks and their silent love for this place.

Like many of the Catholic place-names of California, Spanish explorers named the Santa Lucia Mountains in the 1500s. The region has a much deeper history, however, as the home of the Esselen and Salinan peoples. Before colonization, they lived on the Big Sur coast seasonally. Acorns, game, and sea life were their sustenance. Frequent burning and selective protection of various plant species shaped the landscape into a diverse food system.[38] With the establishment of the Franciscan mission system, these peoples and their lifeways were devastated by disease and frequent massacres. Weakened by conquest, many were forced into slavery at the Missions of San Carlos, Nuestra Señora de la Soledad, and San Antonio de Padua. The 450 or so descendants of the Esselen and 600 or so descendants of the Salinan peoples have yet to be federally recognized as tribes.[39]

In 1848 California became the thirty-first state in the U.S. after the Mexican-American War, and many Anglo families soon moved to the area as homesteaders. By the late 1880s, Lime Creek was being mined by the Rockland Lime and Lumber Company, which was supplying lime for the construction of San Francisco.[40] The supply of ore and wood lumber soon ran out, however, and the land was left mostly abandoned.

Today the hermitage maintains good relations with the Esselen Tribe through the Four Winds Council, a consortium of the four nearby centers of spirituality on the Big Sur Coast. In addition to the Esselen people, the council is made up by the Esalen Institute, a personal growth and gestalt psychology retreat center, Tassajara Zen Monastery, and the New Camaldoli Hermitage.

As I learned, the monks have a reverent if somewhat romantic view of the original stewards of their land. Brother Michael, for example, once shared with me that the Esselen and Salinan peoples "had an amazing way of reverencing nature. If they killed a beast they would apologize to the beast, so we try to carry on some of that harmony with wilderness." The monks take their responsibility as stewards seriously. Since at the least the late 1980s, they have attempted to manage the property as a wilderness preserve, prohibiting hunting, fishing, and most tree cutting.

∾ ∽

The sun had crested from its zenith and was slowly plunging toward its dark resting place in the Pacific. The eucalyptus trees, a flammable import from Australia, filled the air with a dusty tonic. Looking at my watch, I realized I needed to get to the chapel if I wanted to attend Vespers, so I turned around and headed back the way I had come. The Liturgy of the Hours was a kind of flaxen tether that draws the entire community into its inner sanctum to worship God, and as I hurried back, I began to feel its subtle tug.

Entering the chapel, the air was cool, and my eyes slowly adjusted to the low light. In the hallway, a serene Byzantine icon of Mary was illuminated by a single candle peacefully flickering in mellow praise. The seating was arranged in a rectangular foyer with rows of facing chairs, one for monks and one for visitors. The chapel itself was circular, and we only entered it during the Eucharist. It felt like a sort of aboveground Puebloan kiva, a round yurtlike structure with a single hole in the roof. The angular dome was crested by a wooden skylight, and the sun traced abstract patterns across the white stucco walls and rust tile floors.

I took a seat in the back and flipped open a well-worn prayer book to what I hoped was the right page…Vespers…Tuesday. The monks entered in serene quiet, and I stood up at the cue of several reverent retreatants. One of the monks called out an antiphon in an angelic plainchant. The monks responded in a sleepy kind of unison and then bowed to each other, and the first leg of my monastic journey had begun.

Staying Put

Several monks lowered a simple pine coffin into a deep grave among rows of cross tomb markers between the church and the eastern cluster of hermitages. I had arrived at New Camaldoli the day before, and my first interviews were being delayed until Father Bruno Barnhart, a beloved former prior of the community, was laid to rest. The tributes and homilies to Bruno spoke of his sharp intellect, his kind heart, and his affection for trees. The monks were saddened by

*Monks and laity gather for Father Bruno's
interment*

the void he left in the community but almost chipper with convic-
tion that his soul persisted, even as his body now lay covered with
the yellow clay of these chaparral hills.

Bruno will be missed, but his books and talks continue to influence and inspire many who live at New Camaldoli Hermitage and
beyond. Such dense and profound works as *The Second Simplicity*
(1999) and *The Future of Wisdom* (2007) call on Christians to rediscover what he called "participatory knowing," a contemplative practice that sought to go beyond the world-denying Platonism so common among spiritual types. Throughout his career, Father Bruno
pushed for broader ecumenical dialogue, an embrace of the divine
feminine as a response to the overwhelmingly patriarchal heritage

of Christianity, and a deeper engagement with ecological ethics and scientific knowledge.[41] I never got to meet Father Bruno, but it was clear from the monks I spoke with that he had come to deeply love the place to which he had devoted much of his adult life.

And yet every monk has, in a sense, already died. When monks take their final vows, they are declaring their death to the world and their new life in Christ. Like their desert forebears, monks commit themselves to seeking paradise in the wilderness of the human heart. And unlike parish priests or other orders within the Roman Catholic Church such as Franciscan friars, monks (only some of whom are ever ordained priests) vow to live out the rest of their lives attached to a single place.

This commitment is rooted in one of their monastic vows: the vow of stability, from the Latin *stabilitas*, immovable, steady, stable. Their single-purposed lives of prayer are shaped not only by scriptures and monastic history, and by cell, chapel, and refectory, but also by the surrounding hillsides, canyons, groves, and vistas that seep into one's soul over a lifetime.

Having visited the monastery as observers, aspirants who want to test their mettle as a monastic get permission to enter as a postulant, a sort of trial period that usually lasts for four to six months, wherein the monk tries on the monastic life, wearing a simple habit. Then he enters the novitiate, which, depending on the order, can last one to two years. After he completes his novitiate, he professes simple vows and becomes what is called a junior monk, taking a serious try at the monastic life with renewable vows that last another two to three years. During the ritual wherein the monk makes his final vows, the monk lies facedown before the abbot. He is covered with a burial shroud in a ritual that enacts his death to the world and his rebirth into the monastic life. His solemn vows bind him to the community and the place for the rest of his life.

The sixth-century *Rule of Saint Benedict* is clear that the wandering monk, or gyrovague, is, in Saint Benedict's not so humble opinion, not a good monk: "These [gyrovagues] spend their whole lives tramping from province to province, staying as guests in different monasteries for three or four days at a time. Always on the move, with no stability, they indulge their own wills and succumb to the allurements of gluttony, and are in every way worse than the Sarabaites. Of the miserable conduct of all such it is better to be silent than to speak."[42] Stability acts as a counterforce to the fallible human imagination, where the contemplative grass may perpetually appear greener elsewhere.

Just as the monastic disciplines of chanting the Liturgy of the Hours, attending Mass, or receiving spiritual mentorship from an elder monk are essential components of monastic formation, so too is access to and time spent on the usually extensive monastic property. The ability to wander and explore the landscape is essential to working out the kinks and growing pains of a monk's transition out of the world and into the community and the contemplative life.

In his history of the Cistercian monastic order, *Exordium Parvum*, Abbot Stephen Harding (1050–1134) exhorts his fellow monks to become *lovers of the place* and of the Cistercian Rule.[43] Because monks take a vow of stability to the place, the land becomes a kind of spiritual ecology and even an active partner the monks work with during the time of their formation. In many cases, a monk's very identity becomes attached to their chosen order and its history and place where they have vowed to live. Father Bruno lived at New Camaldoli for many decades, and during that time he no doubt became deeply entangled with the community of life there.

This commitment to be lovers of the place through the vow of stability and the process of formation was sometimes even expressed in the language of romantic love. One monk I met stated bluntly, "I just fell in love with the place the first day." This is, of course, not to say that monks' understanding of place is a stand-in for their worship of God, but that the admonition to become a lover of the place gives their home a certain spiritual depth. The monastic sense of place is born out of the ability of land to reveal, reflect, and mediate their experience of God's love and mystic presence. And for many, a sense of place is an essential part of the crash course in "becoming a monk 101."

By the end of the first week, I was getting the hang of the monastic rhythm. After Vespers one night, I sat down at a table with several retreatants. We ate in silence as the prior read from the Rule of Saint Benedict. After my meal, I rolled up my sleeves and walked to the kitchen for my assignment as a dishwasher. Each monk has his work in the monastery, and all share in the chores that keep it running.

I was directed to help wash and dry dishes with two elderly monks who stood washing and drying dishes together at a small sink. They didn't seem to notice my presence because they were taking turns mercilessly sniping at each other over an obscure point of theology. I interrupted, and they turned with unsaintly scowls as I asked what they would like me to do. One monk, who seemed to have been losing the debate, shoved a damp dishrag into my hands and stormed off. The vow of stability also means that a monk is committing to a life lived with his fellow monks. This can sometimes be a challenge. A monastery is a community of imperfect people, living together with all their wounds and problems. This combination, love for the place and love for the community, is the monk's path. A monk tethers himself to place and community, come what may, whether wildfires, floods, earthquakes, or a particularly obnoxious brother.

Spiritual Mountains

Brother Michael adjusted his glasses and approached the lectern with a bundle of notes in his hands. I was just over a week into my visit. His hair was not shorn like many of the other monks, but long, parted on the side, and dark, with salt-and-pepper waves cresting along his half-covered ears. Though the windows of the church were opaque, sunlight was projecting a pale kaleidoscope of shapes across the altar and floor. Michael looked more like a professor than a priest, but his white choir robe tipped the scales. Even though the monks celebrate Mass every day, Sundays are something of a special occasion. Visitors from town attend in greater numbers, and there is a more solemn sense to the liturgy. Brother Michael was preaching, and his sermon was, appropriately enough, about the spiritual symbolism of the hermitage's coastal wilderness.

Brother Michael had been living at the hermitage since the early 1960s and had served as the prior for several years. He began his sermon with an anecdote and then dove into the Old Testament. He preached that the land was not only central to biblical faith; it was also the richly symbolic alphabet with which the Jewish faith was spoken into being. The wilderness was a place of trial *and* encounter for the Israelites as they were liberated from Egypt by Moses. The journey through the wilderness was meant to purify and prepare the Israelites to inherit the Promised Land of Canaan. The towering height of Mount Sinai, its clouded peak, and its location in the desert was a place of theophany wherein the Torah was revealed to the people of Israel through Moses.

The arid and semiarid landscapes and seascapes of the Levant were a spiritual ecology where humanity, God, and land were fused in intimate, reciprocal relationship. The symbols, metaphors, prophesies, parables, and stories that resonated with biblical peoples grew organically out of their experience of dwelling in the erratic biomes of the region.[44] Biblical scholar Walter Brueggemann argues that the land was in fact the crucial expression and affirmation of the relationship between ancient Israel and God. "Land is a central, if not the central theme of biblical faith," he writes. "Biblical faith is a pursuit of historical belonging that includes a sense of destiny derived from such belonging."[45]

Wilderness is one of the most important and prominent features of this biblical spiritual ecology. The word *wilderness*, in the Old Testament, had a much broader definition than it does today and captured a range of socioecological settings: from uncultivated land near a settlement, "the wilderness of Edom" (2 Kings 3:8), to dispersed seasonal pasture lands (Psalm 65:12). Ruins or the desolations of warfare were also wilderness places (Joel 3:19). Wildernesses were places of danger and demons. The ocean, too, with its beast Leviathan (Job 41), was a kind of watery wilderness, a place that threatened to swallow up the world in the primordial chaos-waters of the first chapter of Genesis. The monks of New Camaldoli saw themselves inhabiting that wilderness between land and sea; the tops of the surrounding mountain peaks symbolized their own spiritual ascent toward God.

Brother Michael was enthusiastic for a Catholic homilist, his arms frequently raised to emphasize an important point, ritually adjusting his glasses and then returning his hands to a soft grip on the edges of the podium. After expounding the symbolic power of the mountains of the biblical landscape, he moved into the New Testament. John the Baptist presented himself as the voice crying repentance in the wilderness (Isaiah 40:3).

In preparation for his preaching and wonder-working, Jesus of Nazareth also spent much of his time alone in prayer in the deserts of Galilee and Judea. And the event referred to as the Transfiguration of Jesus on Mount Tabor, Michael continued, symbolically tied his authority to that of Moses on Sinai.

Not only did Brother Michael's rugged homeplace speak to him of God as the creator of all things, but the features of the landscape crackled with the symbolism of biblical mountain and wilderness spirituality. Monastic landscapes are often symbolic landscapes, filled with metaphors pointing to the spiritual journey. The vast ocean, frequent rain, and dense fog symbolized the mystery of God as three persons in one. The trees and flowers, like those in the Psalms, praised God by their very being. What had initially been a beautiful scene was now revealed as a thickly layered symbolic spiritual landscape.

Biologist Terrance Deacon calls Homo sapiens the "symbolic species." This is because we are the only species that makes use of symbols within organized systems of signs such as letters and alphabets to communicate.[46] This is not to say that other species do not use sophisticated signs to communicate, but strictly speaking they do not use symbols. A symbol is generally defined as a mark, character, object, or literary convention that points to or represents something else. The letters on this page represent sounds that come together to form words, which make sense of an idea I am communicating about the concept of a symbol.

The word *tree* is not a tree, but for those initiated into the English language, the characters that spell out the word inevitably *point* to one. A physical tree, however, can *also* be symbolic of various qualities and characteristics associated with it by a particular cultural context. For example, the oak tree is a rich symbol of strength, fortitude, and wisdom in many European cultures, closely associated with pre-Christian sky gods such as Zeus and Odin, because of the tree's curious affinity with lightning.

A symbolic reading of place and landscape has loomed large in social science theories of environmental perception. For example, in their book *The Iconography of Landscape*, geographers Denis Cosgrove and Stephen Daniels define landscape as "a cultural image, a pictorial way of representing, structuring or symbolizing surroundings...a landscape park is more palpable but no more real, no less imaginary, than a landscape painting or poem....[E]very study of landscape further transforms its meaning, depositing yet another layer of cultural representation."[47] From this perspective, land may be the same set of physical objects, but diverse human subjects, identities, and cultures give very different meanings to those objects. Historian Simon Schama says this in slightly different words: "Landscapes are culture before they are nature; constructs of the imagination projected onto wood and water and rock."[48]

As one last example, in Umberto Eco's *The Name of the Rose* (1980), the novel from which I have drawn many of the pseudonyms in this book, the author seeks to make a postmodern point regarding the nature of symbols and the way we make meaning with the world. In the novel, the main character, a Franciscan friar, accompanied by a Benedictine novice, arrives at a cavernous monastery in northern Italy to resolve a dispute between the pope and a group of Franciscans suspected of heresy. After a series of mysterious murders that lead the protagonists into the labyrinth of the vast cloister library, they seek to uncover a secret code embedded in a cryptic document that seems to correspond to the seven trumpets in the Book of Revelation.

While the central character, William, assumes there is a pattern to the murders embedded in the library labyrinth, in the end it is a series of coincidences without inherent purpose or meaning. Interpreters of the novel see it as a commentary on the socially constructed nature of reality: the idea that meaning is culturally constructed and that layers of meaning never actually arrive at some baseline signified referent. Social scientist Michel de Certeau similarly theorized that "we never write on a blank page, but always on one that has already been written on."[49] Symbols and landscape are in constant negotiation with the peoples that live with them. Monks learn to live and breathe the biblical and monastic stories. They internalize the symbolism of the Bible and their spiritual lineages. For many monks, what might represent scenic or natural beauty to some of us invokes a rich symbolic landscape that points the way on their journey to God.

For Brother Michael, steeped in the symbolic landscapes of wilderness, desert, and spiritual ascent, the Big Sur coast was a kind of sacred text that spoke of his own journey to God. He saw symbols of God, spirituality, and monastic virtue everywhere. He ended his sermon with a burst of enthusiasm, smiled coyly, and sat back among his fellow monks, who nodded and sniffed with approval. Enthusiastic retreatants scribbled the last of their notes and then reclined to bask in the homily after the homily, silence.

~: ~

A few days after his homily, I met Brother Michael in the cloister garden for a walk. The air was warm, and large, puffy clouds hurtled through the sky toward the horizon. There was a smell in the air that I can only identify as Californian: equal parts rain, dust, and concrete. Brother Michael was dressed in a denim workers' smock, and his thick-rimmed glasses betrayed a kind intelligence. His hands were clasped calmly behind his back, and he greeted me with

a smile. I stood and shook his hand and thanked him for his homily.
He chuckled softly, shaking off the compliment with humble embar-
rassment and muttered thank you in a low voice.

As we began to walk, he pointed to the garden and said, "Do you
know the symbolism of the monastic cloister garden?" I did but
asked him to elaborate. He explained how monasteries throughout
the ages, especially the classical Carolingian monasteries of the ninth
century, symbolized the Garden of Eden by cultivating gardens at
the center of their monasteries, usually surrounded by walls on all
sides (cloistered).[50]

In the Bible, the paradise-garden motif expresses the tumultu-
ous cycle of Israel's exile and return. This motif begins, of course,
with the second chapter of Genesis, which locates our primordial
parents in a garden of trees planted by God at the beginning of creation: "And the Lord God planted a garden in Eden, in the east, and
there he put the man whom he had formed. Out of the ground the
Lord God made to grow every tree that is pleasant to the sight and
good for food, the tree of life also in the midst of the garden, and
the tree of the knowledge of good and evil" (Genesis 2:8–9, NRSV).
In Latin translations of the Hebrew Bible, *garden* in Genesis 2 is
translated as *paradisum*. The word *paradise* derives from the Persian
word *apiri-daeza*, which described a walled-in orchard or a parklike
area built for the exclusive use of royalty. In the Hebrew world, the
original garden was a place of harmony with nature, abundance of
food and water, and intimacy with God. This motif, of a primordial garden or golden age, appears among other Semitic cultures and
Greco-Roman myth, from Assyrian and Babylonian origin stories
to Homer's *Odyssey*. In Virgil's *Aeneid*, for example, the Elysian
Fields are an earthly paradise-garden in which Aeneas goes "to the
happy place, the green pleasances and blissful seats of the Fortunate
Woodlands."[51]

New Camaldoli's garden was not cloistered, but with its lush
subtropical flora and bubbling fountain, it tied the entire campus
together. And while New Camaldoli's central garden had a long
history within monasticism, it seemed clear that for the monks the

Ventana Wilderness which surrounded them was far more Edenic than any symmetrical cloister plaza garden. Echoing the insights of nineteenth- and twentieth-century nature writers like Henry David Thoreau or David Brower, Brother Michael seemed to be saying that the wilderness *was* the garden.

We began to walk slowly along the monastery's paths with no destination in mind. The surrounding landscape loomed large, its shaggy hillsides bedazzled in sunlight. Brother Michael told me about his doctoral work and reiterated many aspects of his sermon: "Mountains and trees, the ocean and water are incredibly *archetypical*. They are there in all the great religions, and you can even trace salvation history and scripture through mountains!"

"Oh?" I said. "How is that?"

He pointed to an invisible peak and said, "Well, it starts out with Abraham going up a mountain with his son to sacrifice him. And then Moses going up the sacred mountain of Sinai, and Elijah going back to the mountain."

Brother Michael paused to let the arc of his story settle and said, "Oh, and then Jesus's first sermon is the Sermon on the *Mount*—he's the new Moses! Then the Transfiguration of Jesus on Mount Tabor and Mount Calvary and then the Ascension, et cetera, et cetera."

He smiled as I scrambled up this symbolic topography that I had never connected, even in my own familiarity with the Bible growing up going to Sunday school.

"What about the mystics?" I said.

He looked at me with an I'm-glad-you-asked kind of smirk, and said, "So, mountains in their strength and their aspiring upward; the mystics, John of the Cross (1542–1591) talks about the *interior mountain*, and usually we are on the base in the villages and towns working on this or that, but to ascend to the mountain to get to the summit—that's what the spiritual life is about!"

Brother Michael stopped suddenly, bent down, and looked deeply into a cluster of small, white flowers that lay unpretentiously under the flare of a cluster of gaudy bird of paradise. After a few moments of rapt silence, he picked one, turned toward me, and said reverently,

"Thérèse of Lisieux, one of the mystics, she says God has need of the glorious big flowers, but also the tiniest flowers."

Thérèse of Lisieux (1873–1897), a French Carmelite nun who died of tuberculosis, liked to refer to herself as *the little flower*, in comparison to the great and showy flowers of the Catholic mystical tradition like her namesake, Teresa of Ávila (1515–1582). For Brother Michael, whenever he saw small flowers, he was reminded of the simple theology of a spiritual giant who died before the age of twenty-five.

Returning from our walk and wrapping up our conversation before Vespers, Brother Michael said he wanted to show me his hermitage garden. As he unlatched the gate and we entered, he smiled and said, "Here it is!" I was looking at a tangle of weeds and sprawling ivy vines. I looked up at him, intrigued. He laughed and nudged me with a wink. "It's my own little wilderness area," he said. "Weeds are in the eye of the beholder, you know."

Lessons Written in Place

Brother Brendan believed in demons. Like the desert fathers before him who charged into the desert wilderness to do battle with their demons, Brenden found himself following in their hallowed footsteps. He felt that he, too, had won some significant battles at New Camaldoli. As we walked, the faint whoosh-crash of the ocean below came into range, and sea-sky blue spread into full view. Brendan was relating to me the power of the cell. In larger monasteries, the cell is the monk's room in the cloister, but at Camaldoli, each monk had his own stand-alone hermitage.

The spirituality of the cell is a way of talking about how the monks wrestle with their demons. "The cell can be a paradise and perhaps an image of the Garden of Eden, but it can be hell, because it's going to take you to the depths of who you are. It's going to take you into your deepest darkness. If you don't confront that and face that, the cell's going to spit you out, and we've seen that happen with many people. It's also the place, as the desert fathers tell us, where you go to meet the demons."

Jerome (347–420), an early desert father and translator of the Latin Vulgate version of the Bible, remarked "the desert loves to strip bare," and for Brendan, the stark beauty of place but also the discipline of solitude in the monastic cell was an acid bath for the soul. Each of the Camaldoli monks had committed a refrain by their founder Saint Romuald (c. 951–1025/27) to memory: "Sit in your cell as in paradise." And Brendan had done his share of cell work.

On our way back from the view over the ocean, Brother Brendan and I strolled through a cluster of buildings that would lead us through the main campus of the hermitage. It was bright but cool, and we were in no rush as we got to know each other. He was in early middle age and tall, with excellent posture. He had well-groomed brown hair that was parted on the side, with a little gray around the ears. He wore no glasses, and if he had not been wearing a monastic habit, I might have assumed he was a banker or a Wall Street lawyer.

Brendan was born on the East Coast and had worked in a parish setting for many years. The constant activity began to hollow him out, and eventually he found himself discerning a shift in vocation. He visited several other monasteries but found Camaldoli's solitude and silence nourishing to the inner work to which he felt called.

Despite his emphasis on inner work, Brother Brendan also had an abiding love for the place. When I asked about the symbolism of the Psalms, which he chanted each day, he blurted out, "The mountains that melt like wax!"

"What?" I said, a bit taken aback.

"The mountains that melt like wax is a phrase from one of the Psalms.[52] I have been here through a number of El Niños and bad storms, and the mountains melt like wax, literally!" he said, and chuckled.

"I remember another time it was raining so hard, and just as we sang something about the rain and the showers, this torrent opened up. We were in the chapel. It was on a Sunday morning. Everybody just looked at everybody! Just what we were singing, it was happening!" He beamed.

Like Brother Michael, Brendan was literate in the vast, lushly symbolic imagery of the Psalms. For Brother Brendan, the mountains of the Psalmist merged with the mountains of the Santa Lucia range, and the experience of chanting the Psalms during a storm connected them in his mind from then on. The imagery of the Psalms clothes the place with its symbolism and forms a kind of template with which the monk interprets his surroundings.

I asked Brendan if he had any other memories he could share. He thought for a minute, then stopped suddenly and turned toward me. He seemed to have remembered something. In fact, there was a place that reminded him of a very powerful spiritual lesson that he returns to often when he is feeling discouraged. About ten years earlier, he had been called into what promised to be a very difficult meeting, and he related the story with a short theological preface: "I really believe God lives within me, and I remember being in my cell going down to the office for this meeting. It was during the day, and I remember just saying, 'Okay, God, just be with me, God,' so you know here I am believing God really lives within me and my prayer was God be with me. I got to a certain spot, and I could take you back to the place where it actually happened, and I heard God saying, 'Wait a minute, I just want *you* to stay with *me*.'"

Brother Brendan slowed as he said "you" and "me," pointing to himself and then toward the sky. When he walks past or near the place, he inevitably thinks of this significant spiritual lesson that God is with him always, it is we who are distracted or not paying attention. This powerful lesson had been attached to the place and became for Brother Brendan a feature of his own moral landscape.

Sense of place, then, is not just conjured from the symbolic vocabularies we carry in our imaginations and cast like a spell upon the surface of the landscape. Place attachment is also forged from the raw experiences we have with our places. Geographer Yi-Fu Tuan calls this propensity for attachment "topophilia," from the Greek *topos*, meaning place, space, or region, and *philia*, meaning affection or fondness.[53] As monks, or anyone for that matter, spend more time in each place—a home, a chapel, a park—it becomes more and more ingrained in their lives, and they attach themselves to those places. For example, anyone who has been through a breakup might recall how different the city feels in the absence of their significant other. First dates, anniversary outings, and memorable gatherings swell with significance and nostalgia. Place attachment invokes memory, lesson, and symbol but can also trigger the traumas that live in our bodies, not just our symbols of spirituality. In other words, sense of place is an embodied semiotics as well a symbolic landscape, semiotics being simply the study of signs and symbols.

I thought a moment and related this to my own life. It wasn't always the beautiful places that stuck in my memories. After a significant breakup a few years back, my familiar city became an excruciating grief-scape. Places that hardly ever registered felt like rubbing alcohol being poured into my healing wounds. While Brother Brendan's memories related to a deep realization of presence that nourished his spiritual life, attachment to place can also happen through trauma and grief.

For French philosopher Maurice Merleau-Ponty, bodies mediate our experience of the world. Phenomenology, the branch of philosophy concerned with experience, refuses to restrict our subjectivity to the mind. "As I contemplate the blue of the sky," Merleau-Ponty writes, "I am not set over against it as an acosmic subject; I do not possess it in thought, or spread out toward it some idea of blue.... I abandon myself to it and plunge into this mystery, 'it thinks itself in me.'"[54] This approach extends human consciousness out into the world, which simultaneously envelops and composes it. In other words, we are body-subjects, intersubjective agents, the world worlding through us. Our eyes are the eyes of the earth gazing at itself, as anthropologist Richard Nelson once wrote.[55]

This means that the environment (literally that which surrounds us) participates in our perception of it by what it affords, or presents, to our consciousnesses.[56] Anthropologist and philosopher David Abram summarizes this mutuality between body and world when he writes: "To touch the coarse skin of a tree is thus, at the same time, to experience one's own tactility, to feel oneself touched by the tree. And to see the world is also, at the same time, to experience oneself as visible, to feel oneself seen....We might as well say that we are organs of this world, flesh of its flesh, and that the world is perceiving itself through us."[57] Brother Michael's little flower was symbolic of Thérèse of Lisieux, but its color, size, and fragility also shaped the way he was able to interact with and interpret it.

In anthropologist Keith Basso's seminal work *Wisdom Sits in Places: Landscape and Language among the Western Apache*, he shows how stories are attached to Western Apache places.[58] In Western Apache, many place-names are composed of descriptions of a place's most prominent features. For example, the place T'iis Cho Naasikaadéhen translates as "Big Cottonwood Trees Stand Here and There." One story recounts how a Pima woman was killed at this place when she went to check on her daughter soon after her marriage to an Apache husband. In Apache custom, it was taboo to visit one's kin too quickly after a marriage, and as a result her death was attributed to a lack of respect for protocol. This story and its lesson about cultural protocols became part of the place. In a contemporary setting, the moral of the story can be invoked as a powerful teacher simply by speaking the name of the place to someone who may need a lesson in propriety, etiquette, or personal boundaries.

The spot in the middle of the hermitage campus where Brother Brendan had his epiphany about God's presence in his heart is not symbolized by any specific feature; it is embedded through a kind of body-memory invoked by traversing a place of personal significance. The experience has been attached to the place, and now the lesson written in place reads its lesson to him each time he traverses its hallowed mundanity.

~: :~

Standing at the top of the Hermitage drive, one can see the many slumps and slides that plague the clay slopes of the Santa Lucia Mountains. Mudslides have cut off Highway 1 or damaged the hermitage's winding mile-long driveway on several occasions before and since this writing. When it rains, the muddy hillsides seem to melt like earthy wax. Brother Brendan's work in the cell was held by the place, and many of the lessons he has learned over the years are attached to the pathways and vistas of the hermitage landscape. Living on the Big Sur coast is not always easy, but the monks who call New Camaldoli Hermitage home, who have taken vows of stability to seek God in this place, would never dream of leaving.

A Canyon Walk

Brother Adso and I set out from the cloister garden to explore Limekiln Creek, east of the hermitage at the bottom of a steep canyon. He was dressed in casual clothing and a black beanie rather than his monastic habit, yet he somehow still looked like a monk. Perhaps it was the way his black beanie sat cocked back on his shaved head? Or his baggy hoodie, which looked a bit like a cowl?

Brother Adso is a brilliant intellect and a talented musician. His fluency in the concepts of Christianity, Buddhism, and Hinduism were sometimes as hard to keep up with as his pace. Arriving at the rim of the canyon, we were almost level with the tops of a grove of ancient redwood trees sunk into the valley below. The air was perfumed with the scent of laurels, and songbirds chirped and warbled. Brother Adso affectionately recounted stories of wildlife he had come across on his walks, a cougar in the distance, his love for the circling red-tailed hawks. He had come to Camaldoli in the 1990s after being ordained a priest in California. He was drawn to the order for its affinity with Eastern spirituality and its emphasis on silence. He had recently inherited an important leadership role at the hermitage, and the prospect of the additional responsibility seemed to weigh on him.

Brother Adso believed that the simplest definition of a monk was someone rooted in place, and as we descended the steep incline he said, "That's what monks are, they are people who love the place where they live. They sink deep roots into the place where they live." Despite the risk of wildfire and landslide that beleaguered the central coast, he could hardly imagine living anywhere else.

A recent fire had toppled several giant redwood trees, so the already steep trail had to be rerouted down an even steeper incline. We made our way down in halting steps. Perched atop one of these cinnamon leviathans, Brother Adso continued, "We actually go backward and make ourselves slaves to the land and to the place and find freedom there instead of working the land to be free of it to get our independence. We become slaves of the land; I love that. And even the idea of stability, I'm going to stay here. I'm not going to go anywhere else. There's a certain kind of indentured-ness about that, but it's freely chosen in a Wendell Berry kind of way."

Peculiar to any modern sense of individual freedom, the monastic vow of stability reinvents a kind of voluntary landedness. While slavery is an abomination of human oppression, I do not think Adso's reference is in any way directed toward the American experience. Adso, steeped in Italian history, seems to be referring to a kind of chosen indenture to the land that becomes what he called a *"palestra de libertad,"* or playground of spiritual freedom, a paradox that most certainly lands askance among contemporary ears.

Adso's invocation of Wendell Berry's agrarian devotion shows that his sense of place is also keenly aware of the importance of proper care for place. Berry's agrarian sense of place rallies against the excesses of industrial agriculture and consumer capitalism that are ravaging the planet. The monks of New Camaldoli Hermitage have engaged with this brand of environmentalism since the late 1980s, when they declared their property a wildlife sanctuary and prohibited any kind of hunting or harvesting on their property.

I followed Brother Adso as we continued our descent to the bottom of the cool canyon. At one point we had to use a rope to scramble down a section of the trail because several large redwoods had fallen across the switchback. After a few moments of silence, and seemingly out of the blue, Brother Adso said, "You're going to quote for me 1 Kings 19, aren't you?"

When I admitted I didn't know what exactly 1 Kings 19 referred to off the top of my head, he began to paraphrase it. "Elijah in the cave. The Lord was about to pass by, and Elijah sat in this cave and there was a great wind, but God was not in the wind; and there was a firestorm but God was not in the fire, and then there was—"

He paused. "What was the third one? Fire, wind, and…There's an earthquake! God was not in the earthquake! Those are all things that happen here."

He laughed as we continued, and I reflected in silence on his symbolic connection between the biblical story of Elijah and the California landscape of earthquake, fire, and rain. We stopped for a moment to catch our breath. The chaotic California weather and the background threat of earthquakes reminded Brother Adso of the story of Elijah and gave the story a deeper significance. His knowledge of the Bible was not just about theological trivia; the symbolism and motifs spilled out onto the landscape, and the landscape bled into and blended with the biblical symbols.

Stopping, I moved in close to a massive trunk of an impossibly tall redwood tree. They were blackened for several yards above the ground, charred from the most recent fire that swept through the canyon in 2016. Peering into the furrows without touching the sooty bark, I could see tiny cinnamon cracks of fresh bark pushing through as the trees' cambium outgrew the charred bark that bore the brunt of the flames.

Brother Adso reached a large, glassy pool in Limekiln Creek and sat down. He seemed to have known right where it was, and right where to sit. I shed my backpack and decided to wash my hands and sweating face in the cool water. The air was fresh, and the sound of the creek was soothing. He told me that whenever he was feeling low or in need of solace, he would come to this pool in the creek at the bottom of the canyon. We sat for a while talking about the Psalms, climate change, and the challenges of living in community.

After a brief lull in the conversation, Adso pointed to a plant that colonized the ground in circular clumps. He bent down, picked one, and said, "When it closes back in like this, you know it's time to go back up." The plant he pointed to was a species in the wood sorrel family that has three heart-lobed leaflets, like clover. At night, the

leaflets droop and fold in half lengthwise. For Adso, this diurnal
habit was a symbolic reminder that it was pushing toward dusk.

Picking a stalk, a flood of childhood memories came back to me
from my days in elementary school in Southern California. We used
to call a related plant, which lined the hillsides with delicate, bright
yellow flowers, "sour grass" and chewed on the stalks during recess.

Unlike the story of Elijah, the association Adso made with wood
sorrel and the coming dusk was not a symbol extracted from the
Bible used to interpret landscape. Rather, the association had been
formed through an *experience* with place, much like Brendan's reminder of God's presence, or the Western Apache's landscape of
potent place-names.

The *place* holds our memories as much as our minds do. This
means that symbols and experiences are both just as vital to forging
a sense of place. Monastic and biblical motifs, symbols, and meanings form only part of the monastic sense of place, the remainder of
which is woven into the fabric of the land itself and mediated by the
monk's own explorations, memories, and stories.

As we stood and stretched, I picked a stem of sorrel and folded
it into my notebook. Brother Adso was already a ways ahead, so I
trotted toward him and we began making our way back up the steep
grade through slanted rays of dusky light toward the hermitage. ⋅

To Blossom as the Rose

NEW CLAIRVAUX ABBEY

> To be rooted is perhaps the most important
> and least recognized need of the human soul.
>
> SIMONE WEIL

It was still dark as I walked to the early morning Office of Vigils from New Clairvaux Abbey's guest house. The February night was cool but not cold. The moon had set around the time I went to sleep, and the dark sky was skirted by a soft glow beyond the orchards and the tiny town of Vina, California. My feet crunched the gravel of the monastery path, and I heard the waking chirps of a robin, the crazed warble of a wild turkey, and the tender screech of a nighthawk. The muted accordion of frog song hummed in the irrigation ditches, and I could hear the faint thrum of early morning commuters on the distant I-5 freeway.

As I approached the abbey church, the monastery bells began to ring, and their knell seemed to echo through the whole world. Even though it was early, I felt invigorated. I entered the dim church and sat in my assigned stall where two statue-still monks sat in silent repose. One came to life and leaned over gently to help me find that morning's Psalms and which books contained the seasonal antiphons and responsories. The abbot rapped a blunt tap on his choir stall and we stood. The cantor chanted the opening refrain, "Oh God, come to my assistance!"

We replied, "Oh Lord, make haste to help me!"

Bowing in slow unison, we continued, "Glory be to the Father and to the Son and to the Holy Spirit, as it was in the beginning, is

Tree-lined path leading past the vineyard to the New Clairvaux Abbey's chapel

now, and ever shall be, world without end, amen." This trinitarian doxology is chanted at the beginning of services and between psalms.

We then chanted Psalms 45 and 86, each side of the choir alternating in call and response. We sat in silence. The abbot again tapped, and we rose. A monk approached the lectern and read a passage from Paul's Letter to the Romans. Silence. Then a monk intoned an antiphon, and we sang a responsory:

> How gracious is the Lord, and just;
> our God has compassion.
> The Lord protects the simple;
> I was brought low and, and he saved me. (Psalm 116:5–7)

A faint buzz as one of the monks adjusted his hearing aid, a creaky chair, a cough, silence. Receiving a blessing from the abbot, the monks filed slowly out of the chapel in silence, bowing toward the altar with dutiful habit. I reorganized my hymnals and psalters for the next office and walked out into a purpling morning and back to the guesthouse for breakfast, followed by Lauds, Mass, and several interviews with the monks of this holy place.

~: :~

I was met at a cement fountain stocked with koi fish outside the refectory by an eager young monk named Brother Magnus. He handed me a small folder containing the monastery schedule and shook my hand with gusto. His hair was dark and short, and he wore a pair of glasses that reinforced his role as the abbot's secretary. His gleaming white cassock and black scapular, typical of Trappists, was crisp and clean, hinting that his work was mostly conducted indoors. He invited me to follow him and, without looking back, began briskly walking a well-trodden path through the cloister arboretum.

New Clairvaux Abbey is a Cistercian Trappist monastery founded in 1955 by monks from the motherhouse of the Abbey of Gethsemani in Kentucky. The campus comprises some six hundred acres of Central Valley farmland. The monastery is surrounded by orchards to the south, the small village of Vina to the east, and Deer Creek to the north and west. Deer Creek's meandering path empties into the Sacramento River, the largest river in California, running four hundred miles from headwaters to shining sea.

The Order of Cistercians of the Strict Observance (ocso) are descended from the eleventh-century monastic reformer Robert of Molesme (1028–1111) in Citeaux, France. New Clairvaux Abbey is named after Clairvaux, France, where the order's most influential abbot, Bernard of Clairvaux (1090–1153), founded the second Cistercian monastery. The movement surged in the twelfth century across Europe as thousands sought a more authentic and rigorous monasticism compared to that which was being offered in the dominant Benedictine abbeys of the time.

The moniker Trappist came from yet another reform movement spearheaded by the Cistercian abbot Armand Jean le Bouthillier de Rancé in 1664 in the village at La Trappe, France. Eventually, Cistercian foundations descended from La Trappe formed into a separate

religious order. Today Cistercians are either of the common observance or the strict observance. New Clairvaux Abbey, in the heart of
the Central Valley, is of the latter.

These "white monks" attempted to return to the simplicity of the
Rule of Saint Benedict by engaging in farmwork. They believed that
by going to the far reaches of European society, they could participate in redeeming the land so that it would, in the words of the
prophet Isaiah, "blossom as the rose" (Isaiah 35:1).

This instinct to redeem the land was not unique to Trappists,
however. Medieval agrarian theology understood agriculture as a co-
operative enterprise between humans, the earth, and God. Monastic
communities often took it upon themselves to aid in bringing the
pagan wilds under the civilizing cultivation of Christianity.

In her important book *Negotiating the Landscape* (2012), environmental historian Ellen Arnold shows how central the biblical motifs
of wilderness and garden have been in grounding monastic spirituality and identity in place.[59] Arnold's study focuses on a Carolingian-
era monastery complex in Stavelot-Malmedy, located in the forested
Ardennes region of Belgium, which thrived between the seventh
and ninth centuries.

Saint Remaclus (?–671), who founded the monastery in 650
CE, declared that it was established in "a place of horror and solitary isolation which abounds with wild beasts."[60] In their founding
documents, Stavelot-Malmedy is portrayed as being set in a rugged
wilderness that was redeemed through the hard physical and spiritual labor of the monks, who saw themselves as the heirs of desert
hermits like Saint Anthony.

As Arnold shows, however, the Ardennes had in fact been spo-
radically settled and cultivated for many hundreds of years and was
not all that far from established trade and transit corridors. Saint
Remaclus's suggestion that the area was wild and dangerous ap-
pealed to the powerfully biblical themes of fleeing the world for the
desert wilds as the hermits had done before them. The community's
foundation stories exaggerated the remoteness, sparseness of the

population, and pervasive presence of danger to cast themselves in the light of wilderness sowers of both word and seed.

Reflecting on the foundation of Citeaux, Stephen Harding, the author of the early Cistercian history *Exordium Cistercii*, calls it "a place of horror and vast solitude,"[61] a shimmering reflection of the Old Testament book of Deuteronomy. The early Cistercians emphasized the wildness of the place no doubt because they found themselves living within the biblical and early monastic stories; the pagan or remote forests of Europe were their deserts. Another early Cistercian, William of Saint-Thierry (1075–1148), saw this when he compared the monastic reformers directly to the Desert Fathers and their landscape:

> I was amazed to see as it were a new heaven and a new earth, and the well-worn path trodden by the monks of old, our fathers in Egypt, bearing the footprints of men of our own time.... There was a sense in which the solitude of that valley, strangled and overshadowed by its thickly wooded hills, in which God's servants lived their hidden lives, stood for the cave in which our father Saint Benedict was once discovered by shepherds—the sense in which those who were patterning their lives on his could be said to be living in a kind of solitude. They were indeed a crowd of solitaries. Under the rule of love ordered by reason, the valley became a desert for each of the many men who dwelt there.[62]

The well-worn path of monastics seeking secluded "desert" locales connected past and present through place. By framing their surroundings as wilderness, they not only affirmed their monastic identities as spiritual seekers who flee from the world; they also set themselves up as redeemers of the land, shepherding it from forest wilderness to cultivated paradise.

∾ ∾

As I tagged alongside Brother Magnus, the golden California sun felt warm on my skin despite the winter season. The monastery had a parklike feel, and the community largely retained the California rancho style layout the monks had inherited. As we moved between the buildings, I was struck by the beauty of the trees. Over the years, the monks have planted redwood, stone pine, Atlas cedar, and Italian cypress. Several of the black walnut trees are more than a hundred years old. One ancient wind-fallen black walnut tree was going to be milled on site for use in the construction of some new choir stalls.

When the first generation of monks arrived in Vina in the 1950s, the land had been under cultivation for many generations, and there were no illusions of wresting the place from the wilderness. That had been done by the drawn-out conquest of North America by European settler-colonists.

Originally, the valley was the homeland of the Wintu, Yana, and Nomiski peoples, who were driven onto reservations at gunpoint. After being annexed from Mexico in 1850, California was settled through savvy marketing campaigns that promised a lush agricultural paradise. Westward expansion was fueled by a conscious Christian agrarianism that sought to make the grassy desert blossom as a rose. This sentiment was inseparably fused to the Manifest Destiny of American nationalism.

The first European settler to cultivate the property was the Danish American prospector and rancher Peter Lassen, who purchased it from Spanish land granters who had mostly grazed cattle. Lassen planted the first vineyard in the area. Early California vintner Henry Gerke, who purchased the property next, gave the town of Vina its name, and the property was later incorporated into Stanford University founder Leland Stanford's nearly 55,000-acre winery. Stanford planted inappropriate varieties for the climate, however, and quickly pivoted to producing brandy.[63]

After a tour of what used to be the cobbler's shop, Brother Magnus and I sat for a while on a bench in the cool air of a large shade tree. Birds were singing in the trees overhead, and squirrels bopped about preparing for a winter that would never come. While the abbey is a working farm and the regional landscape is dominated by industrial farming and housing developments, the property is home to a surprising number of critters. Mule deer, migratory birds, mountain lions, and squirrels are common sights. Recently a black bear was seen in the area; it apparently broke into some beehives in one of the monastery's orchards.

Deer Creek and the Sacramento River seem to act as wildlife corridors, and salmon in the river are federally protected, a move that has caused local farmers to protest the increasing water restrictions needed to keep the rivers cool enough for salmon.

The monastery is also home to some fifty turkey vultures and about as many wild turkeys, which have taken up residence in the cloister arboretum. In the evenings, the turkey vultures circle the monastery and descend to roost in the trees as predictably as the monks to their choir stalls. It is quite a spectacle, and I never tired of watching it.

Walking behind the cinderblock retreatant quarters, beyond the cloister arboretum, Magnus and I explored a dilapidated but still bright red barn. When the monks purchased the property, the barn was used to house a dairy operation. After several unprofitable years in a row, however, the community converted the dairy and pastureland into prune and walnut orchards that have remained the mainstay of their land use and revenue ever since.

As Brother Magnus rattled off the past and present uses for the monastery's many structures and buildings, I began to see just how much farming has changed over the years. Magnus spoke with an audible disappointment. "Going out to the orchards has always been the biggest thing for us from the beginning up until very recently," he said. "In the last five years we had someone do contract work for us, because we couldn't keep it up and it's more an agribusiness. The old family hobby farm doesn't work today, and if you don't keep up with the new ways of doing things, it just doesn't help."

To begin with, monastic farming was severely impacted by the phasing out of Franklin D. Roosevelt's Agricultural Adjustment Act, which had provided vital price supports and mandatory land idling to keep commodity prices stable. In the 1950s and 1960s this policy transitioned to the payment of direct subsidies for major

commodities such as grain, sugar, and dairy products. Many monasteries were forced to shutter their farms and lease their farmland
to larger operations that had the capital to compete in the changing
agricultural markets.[64] Second, with a steady decrease in vocations,
farming the land even part-time has become less feasible for the
monasteries as the population shrinks and ages. In 2010 New Clairvaux Abbey unanimously decided to hand over day-to-day running
of the orchard to a management company, a difficult decision for the
community.

But the monks' connection to farming was not completely sev-
ered. Heading back toward the chapel for the next office, Magnus
and I passed row after row of newly planted grapevines. In 2005 the
abbey opened a small vineyard that is jointly managed with a Napa
Valley vintner. This development has made the monastery a major
California wine destination, and visits to the tasting room swelled
to twenty-five thousand in 2015. Every year in July, the monks invite
the wider community to participate in the blessing of the grapes,
which involves priestly vestments, procession, incense, and holy
water. This joint venture allows for participation by the monks in
the abbey business but leaves the technical and marketing details to
professionals. Centering the vineyard was a small shrine with two
arching vines and a ceramic icon of Saint Francis of Assisi preaching
to the birds. The westering sun's long shadows complemented his
circular halo and seemed to illuminate the icon from within. As we
walked, the abbey's bells rang out and monks appeared out of nowhere, heading toward the chapel in reverent urgency. Like the gears
of a living clock, the monks mark time with their bodies and voices,
sinking a little deeper into the place they have vowed to call home.

The Resurrection of Trees

When I arrived at New Clairvaux, the branches of the walnut and
plum trees were naked in the dormancy of winter. Even so, Brother
Remigio was worried. With the unseasonably warm winter they
were having, he fretted over whether the swelling plum tree buds

would break too early, leaving them vulnerable to a sudden cold snap that would surely ruin them. As climate change advances, the monks notice that the trees are blossoming earlier. With their leaves gone, the stone-still trees in their rows reminded me of the monks in their choir stalls.

Brother Remigio is a relatively short monk of Polynesian heritage. After greeting me with a kind handshake, we began walking from our meeting place at the guest house toward the symmetric regularity of the orchards. With hands tucked behind his back, he walked with a bit of a shuffle, his back hunched with age and from years of leaning over a choir lectern. He shared memories of tending the orchard and taught me a short lesson on the proper pruning of plum trees, which, as he pointed out, should end up looking something like the communion chalice. The rich symbolism of fruit-giving trees shaped like a chalice that holds the consecrated wine was precious to his sacramental sense of place. He looked back fondly and with some perceptible sadness on the end of his nearly thirty years as the orchard manager and spoke with pride of what they could accomplish when there were more monks and the average age was a bit younger.

According to Brother Remigio, tending the orchard was, despite the noise of the tractors and the harvesters, meditative work. He could lose himself in the repetitive tasks. On one occasion, he let this meditative aspect get the better of him. Early in the morning he was preparing the soil for planting with a tiller. He was deep in thought when he suddenly crashed the entire rig into an irrigation ditch! Luckily, he was not hurt, and the tractor suffered only cosmetic damage. He smiled and laughed, pointing in the direction of the orchard block where this had happened—a place that surely never let him forget about the embarrassing incident.

Even though it could be draining and difficult, there was a spirituality to farming based on resonances between the agricultural cycle and the liturgical one. His was a *liturgical* sense of place. From its Latin root, liturgy simply means "the work of the people" and describes the full suite of a church's worship services.

As Brother Remigio taught me, there is also a seasonal cycle to the liturgy. Each year, the worship cycle begins with Advent (Latin for "arrival," denoting the four weeks before Christmas) and moves through the seasons of Christmas and Epiphany. The forty days of Lent lead to Easter, which is a variable feast whose date is tied to the lunar calendar of Judaism. After Easter the church moves into Pentecost, when the early Christians received the Holy Spirit as an outpouring of heavenly fire and expressed it through the boisterous speaking in tongues (Acts 2). During the rest of the year, the church moves through what is called Ordinary Time, the rotating dates of holy feasts, saints' days, and memorials.

Comparing the liturgy to a forest, German priest Romano Guardini (1885–1968) wrote that "the liturgy creates a universe brimming with fruitful spiritual life and allows the soul to wander about in it at will and to develop itself there."[65] In other words, the liturgy contains much of its own symbolism, but as Brother Remigio taught me, these symbols are infused with the place where it is carried out. Lifting his arm and waving it slowly across the sky, he said, "You look out from the living area, and during the blossom time this would be all white except the trunks of the trees at the bottom. It's beautiful."

"Wow! That is beautiful. I would like to see that," I said, imagining the bare trees fully clad in the fragrant white blossoms of spring.

Walking past row after row of walnut and plum trees, Brother Remigio continued speaking softly but ever enthusiastic. "Each season has its own beauty, and that's very much part of the spirituality of farming."

"The seasonal aspect?" I asked.

"Yes, each season the trees go to sleep and then come back to life again. They resurrect, bearing fruit."

"That's pretty profound," I said, looking over at his excited face.

His hands settled down and clasped comfortably behind his back again as we continued. "Oh, yes, and quite often we used to have a Mass of thanksgiving after each of the harvests. And usually when it was going to be a thanksgiving for the prune harvest I'd make sure every prune was harvested—every prune counts! You've got to pick them up. They are all a gift from God." The liturgy of the church and the liturgy of the land were woven together in a seamless whole.

Brother Remigio loved to walk, but he couldn't walk as far as he used to. Perhaps reflecting on this, we finished our short walk in silence. Brother Remigio wanted to rest before the next office. For Remigio, tending the orchard was not only a kind of cooperation with God to make the earth blossom and improve, not just a worthy livelihood that fed the world, but also an earthly expression of the church's universal liturgy. Like many of his fellow monks, his sense of place had become synchronized with the rhythms of the Northern Hemisphere's agricultural cycle. Plum trees, with their chalice shape, symbolized the Eucharist, and the annual cycle of budding, flowering, fruiting, harvesting, and dying echoed his understanding of the Christian paschal mystery of the birth, life, death, resurrection, and ascension into heaven of Jesus of Nazareth. Place, season, and liturgy are threads in the same cosmic fabric.

The Hinges of the Day

Following the winding contours of Deer Creek, Brother Adelmo and I ended up at the train tracks. It was early in the morning, and we had just said Lauds followed by Mass. The day was crisp and colder than expected. My jaw quivered a bit with the cold, and I rubbed my arms a little to keep warm.

Brother Adelmo, a young monk of Chinese descent, grew up in Canada, so we chatted a bit about living in Vancouver, the weather, the forests. He wore thin-rimmed glasses and walked with his eyes toward the ground. His back was perfectly straight, and his black-and-white habit bunched around his suede, open-toe Birkenstocks. A tassel from his thick belt swayed as we walked.

Each day cargo trains passed within a mile or so of the New Clairvaux Abbey. I told Adelmo that I was surprised by this. Another brother had taught me that the monks had simply taken the train passing as a reminder to pray for the world, and I asked Adelmo if he did that too. He did.

Reflecting on this, I found it quite moving. Rather than resenting an intrusion into their life of contemplation, the monks enlist the aural cue into the very landscape of their prayers. This suggests that contemplation is not an all-or-nothing kind of experience; that one can only be contemplative in the right place or at the right moment. Contemplation is an invitation to presence, awareness, and prayer, no matter where one finds oneself.

For now, all was quiet, and Brother Adelmo and I were discussing his discernment to the vocation of monasticism. For him, this quite naturally dovetailed with his love for the liturgy. Walking along the tracks, I tried to balance on the shiny rail that guided the train's heavy wheels, stumbling off as focusing on a particular phrase or story made me lose my balance.

The annual liturgical cycle is punctuated by a rigorous daily cycle of work, the offices of the Liturgy of the Hours, personal study, and prayer. As he reminded me, the Liturgy of the Hours is a way to "sanctify the hours of the day with prayer."[66] Each day the monks gather to chant the Offices of Vigils, Lauds, Terce, Sext, None, Vespers, and Compline. Terce and None are often said privately or, for novices, in small groups.

The daily repetition of the Divine Office, which shapes the body and soul of the monk, is also shaped by the contours and character of the place. During the noon office of Sext, for example, they sing: "O God of truth, O Lord of might, who orders time and change aright, who sends the early morning ray, and lights the glow of perfect day." The daily cycle of morning, noon, evening, and night prayer sanctifies the passing of time and honors each hour with awareness of its passing. The liturgy consecrates the hours of the day so that place and time weave together.

Philosopher of place Edward Casey grasped this temporal dimension of sense of place when he wrote, "There is no grasping of time without place....Place situates time by giving it a local habitation. Time arises from places and passes (away) between them. It also vanishes into places at its edges and as its edges."[67] Monks spend each day immersed in chanted liturgical prayer. The Divine Office orients the monks to the liturgical and natural time of the day.

Anthropologist Pierre Bourdieu characterized the daily rhythms we form in a place as *habitus*, meaning the constellation of habits, stances, postures, tastes, and practices that a community develops through the day-to-day routines that make up our lives in the places we spend most of our time.[68] Walking from cell to chapel to refectory to library; walking the land; hearing the bells mark the hours; entering the chapel, dipping one's fingers into the holy water; bowing to the altar; standing and sitting in the choir stall; praying at meals; eating, bathing, reading, studying, etc. Each of these actions is a part of the monastic daily habitus; the unfolding of time is enfolded into a liturgy of place, which then becomes the place of the liturgy.

~: :~

Walking back from the train tracks at the edge of the property, Brother Adelmo and I decided to sit for a while near the abbey cemetery. We sat in the dappled shade of the cloister arboretum, among tall Italian cypresses, girthy redwoods, and massive black walnut trees. I asked Adelmo to tell me more about his connection to the liturgy, the seasonality of it. He smiled and said, "Well, especially during the ordinary season if you listen to the hymns during Lauds, the hymns during Vespers that we sing—they are all drawn from the Middle Ages—those hymns tend to reflect the time of day where the sun comes up. As evening draws near, you have the setting of the sun, and the hymns talk about that in reference to Christ being entombed and rising up the next morning during Lauds. There's that rhythmic cycle that we hear and sing, so that definitely penetrates your soul, and I think those early Psalms were intentionally sung during those, what we call the *hinges of the liturgy*—Lauds, breaking into morning from the night, Vigils into morning, and then Vespers into evening, and Compline completes the cycle."

The hinges of the liturgy are also hinges of the day, the diurnal cycle of dawn, midday, evening, and night. This cycle takes on rich symbolic importance not only contrasting light and darkness, but also in the surrender and return of light as a symbol of Christ, pointing to a time beyond time where the monks hoped to be one with God.

This daily and seasonal rhythm had touched Adelmo so deeply that he felt he had almost become a natural feature of the landscape. Looking out at the graves of his fellow brother monks he said, "You become part of the land. Our vow of stability grounds us. And an image that was really helpful for me was the idea of these trees taking root. You know, we've got thirty feet of topsoil, and the roots go very deep. So that was the image of stability that I had. The longer I stay here, the more I can see myself growing in ways I never thought possible. It's not always easy, staying in one place, but the longer you stay the higher you can reach."

Becoming part of the land means that Brother Adelmo felt he was not living *on* the land but dwelling within it and among its creatures, and an important part of that process of sinking deep roots into the place was participating in the daily liturgies that have unfolded without interruption for more than sixty-five years in this small corner of the Central Valley.

∾ ∽

Entering the dark chapel for the office of Compline later that evening, the final office of the monastic day, I felt my way to my creaky choir stall. The lights were almost completely out, and only a single weak lamp illuminated a distant, dark stone statue of the Blessed Mother. I sat in stillness as another day ended, reflecting on my interviews over the past week or so, and was interrupted by flashes of the stresses and worries that awaited me back in Vancouver. When the abbot rapped his staff, we stood facing the illuminated Virgin Mary, and the monks began to chant from memory the 4th Psalm. I closed my eyes and hummed along. After some readings and silence, the monks chanted in Latin the "Salve Regina," a hauntingly beautiful hymn of praise to Mary. When it ended, they began to leave the church for the silence of the night.

I lingered for a few minutes in the thick, incense-laden darkness of the chapel. I sat still and absorbed the silence of the place, feeling encouraged in my work. In my short time as a researcher I had learned so much about Catholic theology, monastic history, and contemplative spirituality. I got up, bowed to the altar, and emerged into the inky darkness of night where the stars were brightly shining and the turkey vultures were rustling in the stone pines as they too settled in for the evening.

Sacred Stones

A prompt Brother Bernardo and I met at New Clairvaux Abbey's chapel entrance after Mass and decided to walk over to the monastery's recently acquired twelfth-century monastic chapter house from Spain that was in the process of being reconstructed. The elegant structure would become the community's new chapel, and Bernardo wanted to tell me more about the history and architecture of the impressive space.

The monks' current chapel was functional but not built to be particularly beautiful. It had been constructed hastily when the monks arrived in 1955 out of crossbeams and particle board, flanked by opaque yellow glass windows.

A chapter house was where medieval monks would assemble to listen to the abbot give talks or read a chapter of the community rule. The monastery in Spain had built a structure for this purpose, housing the task of internalizing the rule into a single place. The stones found their way to San Francisco when billionaire William Randolph Hearst purchased them and imported them to the United States in the mid-twentieth century. Hearst never did anything with them, and they were eventually donated to the city of San Francisco, but they sat idle in a park for years. In the 1990s the monastery convinced the city to sell them, and with the help of dozens of consultants in arranging and organizing the stones, they set about reconstructing the sacred structure. The stones were something of an eyesore anyway, and it was rumored that a local pagan group was

*A column in the twelfth-century Spanish Cistercian
chapel, which was not completed until 2018*

using a small circle of the stones for their annual solstice celebra-
tions à la Stonehenge. Some of the stones had to be replaced or sub-
stantially recrafted, but the majority of the stones are original to the
twelfth-century chapter house.

In addition to restoring the chapter house, the monks expanded
the chapel and added additional space for retreatants. Architect
David Richen envisioned a brick space that would complement and
blend with the ancient Spanish sandstone. The chapel was formally
dedicated in 2018, several years after my visit.

As we entered the then-unfinished structure, I scuffled through
a vaulted archway and a pigeon burst out of the rafters in a flutter.
The doors and glass windows had yet to be installed, and the floor

was rough concrete without tile, splotched with bird poop and dead leaves. The ceiling was enclosed but unlit. Even in this unfinished state, the pale pink-tan sandstone was arrestingly beautiful. My eyes couldn't help but trace the elegant symmetry of its many vaults and slotted windows. The columns resembled petrified trees spreading into a canopy of perfectly jointed stone. It was a work of master stonemasonry, and its restoration was a modern-day miracle.

Brother Bernardo was a stout monk with large, square glasses. He wore a well-used Trappist habit with patches on the elbows. His scapular protruded roundly at the belly. He was proud of his Cistercian heritage. At the time of the reform, Benedictine abbeys were famous for their wealth and often boasted elaborate decorations, golden altarware, abundant statuary, and intricate stained glass. In Europe, some abbeys used pure gold to decorate their altars, embedded fine jewels in Gospel manuscripts and crucifixes, and adorned chapels with large tapestries and carpets. As one custumal document noted, an Easter service at one Cluniac monastery required nearly five hundred candles.[69]

Cistercian architecture anticipated much of the later Protestant sensibility for simplicity and an emphasis on form rather than detailed decor—quite the opposite of the intricate and gaudy Gothic and Baroque-style churches of the classical medieval and later Counter-Reformation periods.

Pointing out the guild marks in several of the columns, Brother Bernardo reflected on the spirituality behind Cistercian built spaces as his voice echoed a little off the soft stone: "Proportion, beauty, harmony. Space that gives a sense that God must be something like this. It is timeless. You go out to nature that is untouched, and you get the same experience. You go to the national parks and nature is beautiful. There is space, there is a sense of harmony, and to a certain degree there is proportion."

Brother Bernardo saw the space as bringing the beauty and symmetry of nature into the built environment. The monks of New Clairvaux had gone to great lengths to bring a piece of their monastic heritage to the grounds of their monastery. They wanted a space that was not only a cherished memory holder of their spiritual ancestors, a physical embodiment of their monastic identity, but also one that beautifully reflected the sacredness of their daily and seasonal cycles of prayer. Buildings, then, are integral to what makes a monastery a distinct place. As Edward Casey writes, "A building is a place for places."[70]

As places for places, monastic buildings form nodes in the network of daily movement the monastic habitus entails. Monks are constantly moving between cell and chapel, chapel and refectory, and the spiritual ecology of any monastery includes these indoor sacred and quotidian spaces and the pathways that connect them.

Chapel spaces contrast and complement the activities that take place during work, meal, and leisure time. They are an *axis mundi*, a centering point on the land that gives a bearing to all other places and spaces. Chapels also contain the most sacred element of any Roman Catholic edifice, the consecrated Eucharistic host, which is experienced by Catholics as the real presence of Christ within its bready appearance.

Entering any church, but especially monastery chapels, I have been struck by the sudden shift in psychic gears, and even open to the elements and unfinished, this chapel was no exception. The smell of candles and incense, the sudden silence, the vaulted ceilings, all immediately slow me down and draw the eye heavenward. I also find it humbling to know that walls have absorbed the chanting of thousands of days and many generations of monks. They are, as one monk phrased it, containers for the Psalms, which, chanted at the various hours of the morning, day, and night, are themselves richly filled with symbolic pastoral imagery.

Standing near what would become the altar, the most holy place in this holy place, Brother Bernardo told me he believed that these stones, saturated with the prayers of his spiritual ancestors, are sacred. His face shone with the satisfaction of the many sacrifices the community has made to realize their dream. Running my hands over their smooth grain and tracing the tight seams between stones with my thumb, I couldn't help but agree.

The Orchards of Remembrance

Riding shotgun in a dinged-up Ford pickup truck, I sat next to Brother Severinus, who pulled out of the cool brandy cellar that now housed a miscellany of tools and abbey vehicles into the mild winter heat of the California day. Severinus was in middle age, with reddish-blond hair cut short but not quite buzzed. He was wearing his monastic habit with a sweater over the top, and his glasses were pulled down his nose so he could see the road. The plan was to head into the orchard and check on some irrigation lines and then visit a few of his cherished places. He rehearsed the by now familiar history of the Trappists and the monks of New Clairvaux Abbey and talked with pride about the community's land-use plan, which included the recent installation of a solar panel array that would save the community thousands of dollars a year and help them be better stewards of the environment.

Driving along the southern boundary of New Clairvaux's orchard at the pace of a brisk walker, Severinus lamented, "If I were in better health, and we had more time, I would be walking, because then your feet are getting into the soil, the leaves, you're feeling the branches, the weeds, the smells, the birds, the insects, the sun, the shade. You're getting more of the real experience." He was recovering from a bout of pneumonia and had to stop talking to nurse a coughing fit every now and then. I nodded and said it was okay, and we agreed to hop out any time there was something to see or talk about.

It was an overcast day, but the sun still shimmered through a gray blanket of clouds. Even though I had been at the monastery for more than a week and a half, I tried to break the ice a bit more by telling Severinus about my time volunteering in an orchard in Utah and admitted that I found the work to be very difficult, and about how their operation seemed different from the industrial farming I had seen driving into the valley.

Severinus smiled and said, "There's a lot of corporate farming here in California. There, it is an investment. When the prune industry is good, they plant prunes, when it's not good they tear them out and plant something else. It's not that we are not affected by it, and we don't follow the markets, but we're in it for the long haul."

I nodded as we bumped along. Monasticism was a comfortable partner to the orchard, and as I had learned, the cycles of the day and the seasons of the year blended well with their monastic way of life. Being in it for the long haul had been made more difficult by waning vocations and the increasing average age of the community. During the first years of Severinus's formation, the monks spent all their working hours in the orchards, and as a result they often felt a strong kinship with these trees. Just as they pruned the trees to make them more productive, God was slowly pruning away their own imperfections. For Severinus, monasticism, creation, place, and spirituality were a seamless whole bathed in the light of God's grace.

After a few moments of silence, Severinus let flow a musing he seemed to have been sitting with for a few moments. "I think work is not just taking, it's giving as well to the land. It's not just how I can benefit, but how can the land benefit by my care? What must I do so as not to abuse? Because to abuse the land is to abuse creation and is ultimately to abuse me, because I am part of it."

He looked over to make sure I was following and continued, returning his eyes to the road. "There's a day I am going to die, and we still have the old practice here. A monk is buried, no coffin, just buried right into the ground, he's wrapped in his cowl, sits on a little board, but you are just put right into the ground. Our corporal remains become soil, and then a tree takes up the soil and it helps it to grow. We're part of this very natural cycle."

I let the words sink in a bit. Surprisingly, it made me feel a little weary, and I sighed a bit as I looked out the window. I had moved away from my childhood home in 2001 and lived in half a dozen places since. Even though I enjoyed living in Vancouver, I had no idea if I would be buried there. My life, even at thirty-five, was still somewhat transient, and thinking about the idea of home felt distant, refracted through the prism of cherished memories and future aspirations.

Canadian spiritual activist Stephen Jenkinson, who writes beautifully about the problem of belonging to places that have been colonized by the geographically "homeless" cultures of Europe, is cautious to allow sense of place to be *merely* symbolic. "Being at home," he writes, "is having kinship with the place where your kin live and have lived and cooked and loved and suffered their sufferings and known their Gods, the place where they died and were gathered in."[71] The monks of each of the monasteries in this book develop a kind of kinship with the land, and at the end of their days, though their souls long for God, their bodies are laid to rest on the bare soil that nourished them throughout their lives as monks. Having been reborn into the monastic life, they know, within a matter of a few feet, where their mortal bodies will give themselves back to the earth. During the Ash Wednesday liturgy, as the priest smudges ash on the congregants' foreheads, he says, "Remember that you are dust to dust and to dust you shall return."

~: ~

We slowed to a crawl. Pointing through an open window, Severinus said, "Each of these blocks were planted in 1980, the year I entered, so these were just little trees. We would come out every afternoon in that beastly hot summer and hoe the trees."

The blocks had just been pruned for the winter, and branches lay in a raked tangle along the geometric rows of amputated trees. In recent years, the community had been keeping to a more regimented rotation, with orchards being replaced when they began to decline in productivity.

Turning a corner, Brother Severinus jerked to look over his shoulder, despite there being no traffic in the orchard. "You know, it's a little sad," he said, "because we worked these and got to know the trees, and each orchard block has its story."

He pointed out the window past me and said, "This is our oldest current block. I believe this was planted in 1962. So, this block is forty-three years old, and it will probably be around for another five years, but then it gets removed. And something of your soul—I don't want to sound too romantic here—but at least for me, some of my life story is in here." He paused briefly and added, "And then it's gone. Now it might be another prune or walnut orchard, but it's not going to be the same."

He smiled to himself and slowly took on a posture that would do justice to the story that was bubbling out of the dirt we drove past. "One time I was out here, but one of the brothers walking the levies suffered heat exhaustion, I guess. I don't know. Anyway, he just kind of collapsed, and the other brother panicked and brought him in. Meanwhile, he wasn't out here, and the water was running so the levy broke!"

He laughed, looking over to measure my reaction. "Anyway, it raised havoc," he said, a smile lingering on his lips.

Memories of tending the orchard continued to flow like the slow, silent water of the irrigation ditches. We got out occasionally to check a pump, irrigation line, or eroding bank. The orchard blocks still held many of Severinus's memories. As I had learned from Brother Brendan and Adso at New Camaldoli Hermitage, these places are teachers for Severinus, patiently reminding him of lessons learned during the grueling tasks of running an orchard.

Passing what to me seemed like another nondescript block of naked trees, Severinus began to chuckle. "There were a lot of valuable lessons. Out there in the cold or sometimes in the rain, a branch would slap you in the face, and you just want to, you know…you would not want to say pious words in that moment! So, it constantly taught you a lot about yourself, and the trees really were images of you in many ways, what you needed to remove from your life."

Orcharding was an applied theology. Weeding, pruning, fertilizing, each of these farming techniques had a spiritual correlate. The spiritual trees in the wilderness of the human heart were slowly tamed by the nurturing hand of the orchardist, and with luck they bore the fruits of the spirit.

Raising his finger, he stopped, his voice quavering a bit with reverence. "There was kind of a critical moment in my vocation in this orchard. A moment of great purification and I guess you'd say a moment of great trial, but a moment of great grace. It was a very trying moment, kind of a 'dark night' and then epiphany, as it were. Very early on, within a week or so after I entered the monastery. In fact, it took place right in this first row here." He pointed. "I don't even know what I was doing, I know it was October and it was in Benedict Orchard. It was right around here. A very intense moment of purification, and then just a moment of breakthrough and enlightenment."

Severinus was describing a common experience among monks, referred to as *acedia*, or a sort of spiritual lethargy that sets in after a time living the monastic life. John of the Cross wrote of it as a dark night of the senses and of the soul—a time of feeling God's absence. And for many monks attracted to the monastic life, a strong fervor at the outset can fade, and along the way there are many trials to one's vocation. Only a few weeks in, Severinus already felt as though he was just going through the motions, or perhaps that a life outside of monasticism would be more productive, rewarding, or exciting.

His moment of breakthrough is also comparable to Thomas Merton's famous mystical encounter as he was visiting the doctor in 1958. Merton felt a sudden deep connection and sense of belonging to the people around him, who he said were walking around shining like the sun, though they did not realize it.[72] For interpreters of Merton, this experience led him to write more about social issues and war. The experience happened at the intersection of Fourth and Walnut, in downtown Louisville, Kentucky.

Brother Severinus looked down his glasses at me and said, "I guess it was a kind of 'Fourth and *Walnut*' experience, you could say." We both laughed at his dry monastic orchard humor and headed back toward the monastery.

Seeing the Forest and the Trees

OUR LADY OF GUADALUPE ABBEY

For then are they truly monastics when they
live by the labor of their hands.

SAINT BENEDICT OF NURSIA

Brother Patrick had been a monk of Our Lady of Guadalupe
Abbey since 1956. He looked up at me through thick eyeglasses as
he steadied the ladder. I wobbled my way to the top with a small
gas-powered tree pruner. The engine mumbled in my hands as I
steadied myself and extended the handle mechanism to reach the
blade across the top of the hedge that divided the monastic garden
from the book bindery loading area. I began hacking at the prolific
blackberry shoots that were launching out of a laurel hedgerow like
verdant spikey rocket ships.

It was not going well. The blackberry shoots were proving quite
resistant to my parries. I assumed that the saw's ineffectiveness was
due to my own awkwardness, inexperience, and vertical precarity. I
slowly began to realize, however, that in fact something was wrong
with the saw itself; it was just not cutting the way a good chainsaw
should cut.

I killed the power and climbed down the ladder. Patrick and I
splayed the saw out on the ground and began to look it over—perhaps the teeth needed sharpening, or they were getting caught somewhere along the sprocket or bar. I continued inspecting the saw.
Then, with a gasp, I laughed out loud.

Brother Patrick knelt and said, "What is it?"

I pointed at the chain and looked up at him with a smile.

Our Lady of Guadalupe Abbey's chapel through a stand of oak trees

"The chain is on backward!" he roared and laughed a hearty belly laugh. "You won't get much done with that!"

He stumbled away to grab a tool kit from the nearby shed. After righting the chain, and a quick sharpening for good measure, we were back to work, this time making easy progress against the prolific cascade of thorny vines.

∾ ∾

I first visited Our Lady of Guadalupe Abbey, a Cistercian Trappist monastery, in 2013 on my way to Vancouver at the start of my doctoral program. Even during that short visit, I could feel something special in the place, which was nestled against a small rise that ran from north to south in the heart of the Willamette Valley of western Oregon. My thirty-day monastic-life retreat came in 2014, and a year or so later I visited as a researcher, after my stays with New Camaldoli Hermitage and New Clairvaux Abbey. I was excited to be back.

Guadalupe Abbey was founded in 1955 by forty-one monks. Their founding motherhouse has a long history in North America going back to the small Cistercian monastery of Petit Clairvaux in 1825 in Nova Scotia. The monks that founded Petit Clairvaux eventually relocated to Rhode Island in 1900 after two structure fires did extensive damage to the monastery. Our Lady of the Valley, as it was renamed, endured into the 1950s, when it too burned down and the monks once again relocated to their final home in Spencer, Massachusetts. While in Rhode Island, however, the prosperous monastery made several foundations. One delegation was sent in 1905 to Jordan, Oregon, but that foundation failed to flourish, and the monks returned to Rhode Island.[73]

In 1948 Our Lady of the Valley, which was housing more than a hundred monks, decided to make another foundation in Pecos, New Mexico. Though enamored with the site, the monks who were sent to Pecos eventually gave up on the property's farming potential and in 1953 purchased a 1,300-acre property in Carlton, Oregon, not far from the former Jordan foundation. The Abbey of Our Lady of Guadalupe, which took on that patronage in New Mexico, retained the name.

The monks continued farming in Carlton and eventually expanded their operation to include forestry. After the restructuring of the agricultural markets in the 1950s and early 1960s, the abbey closed its farm and began to lease its farmland to local operations. Trying to replace their revenues, the abbey opened a carpentry shop that manufactured church pews and other furniture and then a book bindery that mostly sourced clients from local universities. In the 1980s the abbey added a fruitcake bakery, and in the 1990s a wine storage and labeling facility.

Like New Clairvaux, also a Trappist abbey, farming has been central to Our Lady of Guadalupe's vocation. The entire Benedictine family is well known for seeking to balance work and prayer into a seamless way of life. As soon as a monk joins the monastery, he is put to work. In addition to diving headfirst into a litany of classes on monastic history, theology, and spirituality, and participating in the Liturgy of the Hours, the budding monk is also assigned to monastic work duties within the community.

This monastery work detail can range from cleaning bathrooms, doing clerical office work, taking out the trash, and looking after retreatant reservations to teaching novices, cooking, running errands, repairing and maintaining community vehicles or machinery, fundraising, and manning the bookstore. For Trappists, this work traditionally included land-based work that might have included milking cows, tending chickens, gardening, beekeeping, preserving fruits and vegetables, broad-acre grain farming, and doing forestry. These days, with the average age of monks progressively climbing higher, industries that required manual work have diminished in scale, been delegated to staff, or contracted out.

If place is the *where* of the monastic life, work and prayer are the *how*. The Benedictine motto *Ora et Labora* (work and prayer) orients each monk toward a balanced life of manual labor and prayer that eventually begin to blur together: prayer is sacred work, and work can be offered up as a prayer. The Rule of Saint Benedict devotes most of its seventy-three chapters to the *Opus Dei*, God's work. In chapter four of the rule, after listing the virtues of a good monk, Benedict calls these the "tools of the spiritual craft," and the monastery the workshop within which this craft is to be perfected. The rule discusses the practice of manual labor only briefly, as an antidote to idleness:

> Idleness is the enemy of the soul. Therefore the Brothers should
> be occupied at certain times in manual labor.…And if the
> circumstances of the place or their poverty should require that
> they themselves do the work of gathering the harvest, let them not
> be discontented; *for then are they truly monastics when they live by
> the labor of their hands*, as did our Fathers and the Apostles. Let
> all things be done with moderation, however, for the sake of the
> faint-hearted.[74]

The faint-hearted in Benedict's day were those born to noble blood, not used to working the land, or those priest-monks who preferred copying manuscripts, chanting the Psalms, and celebrating Mass over harvesting grain with a scythe.

The feudal context of *labora* is an important perspective to maintain whenever considering the value placed on manual work by contemporary monastic communities. Medieval European monasteries functioned as small counties, and typically the monks managed their own affairs through a variety of duties.

The monastery cellarer, as they were called, was charged with organizing, supplying, and stocking the monastery with the necessities of life such as wheat, beans, milk, butter, cheese, honey, wax, cloth for habits, sheep- and pigskin for parchment, and timber and stone for building. They supplemented these wares with the produce from their own abbey vineyards, flower and vegetable gardens, fish ponds, herds of cattle, sheep, and bees but still regularly relied on the wider feudal landscape to meet the needs of these often large communities of monks.[75] Lay brothers, landed tenants, or indentured laborers often performed the more strenuous and backbreaking manual labors such as beekeeping; forestry; herding pigs, cattle, or sheep; and planting and harvesting crops.[76]

By the time of the Cistercian reforms of the twelfth century, Benedictine monasteries such as Cluny and its daughter monasteries were performing elaborate high masses and liturgies that took up most of the professed, or "choir," monks' time. The zealous breakaway monks of the Cistercian reform sought to return to manual labor as a foundation for monastic ascetical and spiritual practice.

They also sought to break ties with the manorial (feudal) system by not accepting tenant workers, tithes, or rents. The Cistercians soon realized, however, that *some* division of monastic labor was a necessary evil. Their solution was to employ *conversi* or vowed lay brothers who were organized into granges and lived and worshipped separately from the choir monks, much like the former feudal arrangements.

This situation where monasteries were embedded within the feudal social system shifted after the collapse of the manorial system partially brought on by the Black Death, which radically changed the value of manual labor due to a scarcity of laborers. Further eroding the monastic land base were the impacts of the Protestant Reformation and later the French Revolution, which both drastically reduced monastic land holdings and sent many orders to found houses of refuge in North America.

In fact, the Benedictine motto of *Ora et Labora*, which has come to be synonymous with monks living the Rule of Saint Benedict, is not itself contained in the Rule of Saint Benedict. Seeing work as a virtue-producing spiritual practice did not fuse with monasticism until the nineteenth century, when a modest Benedictine revival spread throughout Europe and rode the wave of Manifest Destiny in North America. What's more, the rise of industrial capitalism, which ignited various Romantic movements throughout Europe, rubbed off onto monastics who framed monasticism's sense of manual work as an agrarian and pastoral bulwark against the monoculture of industrial production, which the monks' regimented time-keeping devices partly inspired.

Regardless of its roots in the manorial system, for contemporary monks in the Benedictine family, including Cistercians, *Ora et Labora* is still a powerful theology of balancing the tasks of daily life with the practice of contemplation. This theology of work can give even the smallest task spiritual meaning. Cistercian monk Father Michael Casey reflects on how the role of work blends with Benedictine spirituality today: "There is a seamless connection between all the activities of the monastic day: liturgy, prayer, reading, working, eating, sleeping, walking, sitting. The 'spirituality' of work is to be found in its harmonious integration in the whole monastic endeavor. There is no autonomous meaning to work: it makes sense only in its positive contribution to a life of prayer and virtue."[77] Daily work not only serves to enrich the spiritual lives of the monks; it also leaves its mark on the landscape itself, forging deeper connections to particular places through memory and moral lesson, as we saw with the monks of New Clairvaux Abbey and as I learned from my time working with Brother Patrick at Guadalupe Abbey.

∾ ∾

After a job well done, Patrick and I carefully disposed of our blackberry cuttings, cleaned our tools, locked up the shed, and stood chatting for a minute about nothing in particular. We headed toward the monastery to clean up and prepare for the midday office of Sext before lunch. I was tired, but the work was satisfying, and besides, what better boss to have than a monk!

The Tree Farm and the Forest

The March rain was holding off, even as dark clouds threatened, but Brother Salvatore and I decided to go for a hike anyway. Salvatore wore a bright yellow raincoat that, with his beard and round eyeglasses, made him look like a scholarly fisherman. We exited the north side of the cloister and began to reveal something of the lives we had lived before meeting. As we moved under the canopy of the forest, the air cooled. Most of the lush Douglas fir forests on the extensive property have been planted, replanted, and maintained by the Trappist monks of Our Lady of Guadalupe Abbey since the 1950s.

As we walked, we passed a large (and somewhat quaint) statue of Jesus who stood with open arms at the head of the trail, welcoming us into the woods. Brother Salvatore crossed himself quietly, and we began to climb the steep grade that dominates the eastern half of the property.

Brother Salvatore and I had ambitions to hike to the small brick shrine to the Virgin of Guadalupe at the top of the monastery's property, which looks out over the patchwork of farm and forest that blankets rural Oregon. We walked and talked at a moderate pace, but with the steep incline we were quickly winded and stopped to breathe. I looked up into the canopy and then down at the ground to see a beetle scurry from a lethargic rough-skinned newt. Salvatore had a painfully shy demeanor but a sharp intelligence and a kind voice. He decided to become a monk at a young age, because he realized that throughout his life God had, as he put it, been looking his way, and it was time for him to start looking back. Despite all the worship they do in church, the forest always felt particularly sacred to him. This was because he felt God's presence in creation. But it

The restored Oregon white oak savanna lays dormant in the gloom of March

was also because the forest held the memory of his brother monks and their tireless work in the forest over the years. For Brother Salvatore, Guadalupe Abbey was home, and he felt grateful for that every day.

∾ ∾

Our Lady of Guadalupe Abbey is located on the traditional territories of several groups of Kalapuya peoples, who were driven from the area by settlers in the 1850s and now belong to the Confederated Tribes of Grande Ronde, though the Warm Springs Tribe, whose reservation is farther east, stewards land near the abbey as well. Much of the area was managed as an oak savanna grassland, kept open by Indigenous seasonal burning practices. Oregon white oak, the predominant oak species, was managed for acorns, and the grasslands supported purple carpets of camas and game such as deer. The collapse of the Kalapuya food systems saw a major reduction in prairie and savanna ecosystems, in some areas by as much as 90 percent between 1850 and the present. Settlers and later the forest industry converted much of the area into profitable grain farms, grass seed farms, hazel orchards, and pasture. The rockier soils and hills were planted with Douglas fir, which tended to overtop the oaks if they were not removed outright.

The previous owner of the property, a farmer and logger, clear-cut the land after he sold it to the community in 1953. The first monks to arrive found a "moonscape of stumps," as one monk put it. This did not deter the monks, however, who moved onto the property full-time in 1955. Soon they began planting trees. They started with a small Christmas tree farm and then began to slowly reforest the uplands by hand.

Eventually the monks were actively working to manage some 880 acres for timber production, planting mostly Douglas fir but also experimenting with ponderosa pine, knobcone pine, hybrid poplar, and Leyland cypress, which was encouraged by local extension agents as potentially profitable in the future.

By the mid-1980s, a small crew of forester-monks planted, thinned, pruned, and harvested all the trees themselves. They would harvest a small block and then replant the area in tightly spaced rows of single species saplings. This "tree farm" approach, promoted by Oregon's extension service and the wider Oregon forestry industry, was designed to maximize the production of timber as a commodity despite the many other species and values that exist in natural forests.

Trappists have always seen themselves as hard workers and desired to live rurally. Over the centuries they have seen themselves as proud stewards of their land, but stewardship also includes the duty to manage the land productively to support the economic needs of the community. For example, one of the abbey historians for the Rhode Island community boasted, "This year, without the help of any engineer, we built a great dam at the point where the stream begins to curve, for the purpose of collecting the water into an artificial lake that will freeze in winter and supply us with ice for the use of the community." Engineers, yes, but Cistercians have never been ruthless exploiters of nature. In New Mexico, as they struggled to farm, another more poetic annalist wrote, "Our amateur botanists are still finding new flowers; they are everywhere in extraordinary profusion, reminding us of their Maker's loveliness and lavish generosity." A no-nonsense pragmatism could always be matched by a deep mystic love for the created world. For centuries Trappists were known primarily as farmers, but after the major reforms that came with the Second Vatican Council in the 1960s, the land-based monks of Guadalupe started to become more interested in conservation than farming.

෴

On a gravel road that had flattened out somewhat, the thick forest obscured the nearby monastery. We began to talk about the land, stewardship, and conservation. Walking by a particularly tidy grid of Douglas fir trees, Brother Salvatore stopped with a smile, pointed, and related a memory about the former forest manager. "Brother Rome, when he was with us, was one of the main planters, and he walked by here once and said, 'This is what some people contemptuously call a tree farm!' At which he took great umbrage because he thought it was a forest."

I spent the summer after my trip to Europe, which included a stop at the Carthusian monastery in Slovenia, as a forester on the seasonal crew at the Yale Forest. Throughout my undergraduate degree studying anthropology, I had learned to observe the cultural landscape. As a forester, I was now much better at understanding the ecological landscape as well. A natural forest has a diversity of canopy layers, a more diverse set of tree and understory species, and many more dead logs and stumps. All this diversity becomes habitat for animals, insects, worms, fungi, and microorganisms that are also part of a forest ecosystem. Since at least the 1980s, forest ecologists and environmental activists had begun to recognize that forest plantations lacked much of this crucial diversity, which was sacrificed for the sake of uniformity, predictability, and profitability.

Brother Salvatore, who came to consider himself something of an ecologist-monk, realized that there *was* a difference between a regenerating forest and an intensively managed tree plantation. Brother Rome, steeped in a production-oriented paradigm where trees are understood primarily as crops, thought the distinction was belittling to the work he and other monks had done to reestablish the forest from the degraded state it was in when they arrived. For Salvatore, the place not only held the memory of Brother Rome; it also marked a cherished lesson about the abbey's commitment to ecology.

We stayed a minute to soak up the curmudgeonly energies that Brother Rome had left behind in the stiff rows of trees. His comments were made while the community was undergoing a major paradigm shift in its understanding of what good stewardship of the forests looked like. An important catalyst to this process had come to Guadalupe Abbey in the late 1980s when a particularly heavy-handed clear-cut near a favored picnic area angered several of the monks, staff, and regular retreatants. After a heated community consultation, it was decided to discern a new forest management strategy by hiring a consulting forester to help implement a more sustainable approach to forest management. In 1995 the forester conducted an exhaustive inventory of Guadalupe's property and collaborated with the community to write a management plan that would balance spiritual values, ecological health, and the need to generate a small revenue. Since then, the abbey has transitioned to an ecological rather than a commercial approach to forest management. Granted, their other industries make this possible, but the community is committed to taking better care of the land in a more balanced way.

The abbey's forest management plan now dictates that patch cuts be no more than two acres in size and that stands which have been too densely planted be thinned to diversify the forests' age and structural diversity. An eighty-acre section of forest has been designated as a remnant old-growth protected area and set aside from thinning and commercial harvest altogether. The management plan also stipulates that harvested areas be left with more standing dead trees and fallen logs for use by wildlife and fungi. The community has stopped the practice of planting nonnative trees and has begun to remove aggressive nonnative species such as false brome, Scotch broom, and English hawthorn.

Encouraged by their consulting forester, the abbey then enrolled in a conservation easement, which is an increasingly common conservation tool for private working lands with high conservation values. An easement comprises a set of restrictions on private property related to conservation values and often prohibits further building, agricultural activities, and subdivision. An easement is usually paid for by a nonprofit organization with an interest in conservation. In this case, Bonneville Power Administration, a hydroelectric dam company on the Columbia River, has been legally obligated to purchase conservation easements for habitat restoration in and around the Columbia River because of the land it flooded by building its dams. After a lengthy process, the monastery received a substantial amount of money to keep the property from further development.

Once enrolled, the forest manager proposed that the abbey restore some areas to oak savanna. Some of the monks were skeptical, as they had grown accustomed to the closed canopy forests they had worked so hard to establish. As the forester patiently explained to the monks, the Kalapuya peoples in the area had managed the rolling foothills of the coastal range of western Oregon for acorn and deer browse with fire. The dry summers made the area ideal for Oregon white oak, but due to European settlement Oregon white oak ecosystems, which support a wider range of bird and mammal species than closed canopy forests do, were nearly extinct in the state.

The abbey tentatively agreed, and with a small crew, the forester painstakingly removed all but the oak trees in the area just above the retreatants' quarters. Then he removed the shrubby nonnative weed species. Finally, the monks planted native grass, forbs, and wildflower seeds. Every couple of years, they walk the site with pesticides and spot spray any returning nonnative species. Since then, bird life has flourished in the savanna, and monks and retreatants alike love the savanna's open structure, where several abbey trails intersect.

Forestry work has undergone a major transformation at Guadalupe Abbey. Like New Clairvaux Abbey, the monks have had to step back from their central role in managing the land and now oversee contractors and consultants. But so too has the *spirit* of land-based work changed at Guadalupe. Today, the monastic community sees itself not as a tree farm but as a nature reserve and sanctuary for the world-weary pilgrims who come on retreat and the abundant wild-life that make Guadalupe their home. The place now pays deference to its own ecological and Indigenous past.

The monastery is one of the largest intact private forest areas in Yamhill County, which, being primarily agricultural, has very few protected areas or walking trails. The conservation easement stipu-lates that the abbey be accessible to the public, and on weekends the parking lot is filled with eager peri-urban hikers who have come to explore the monastery's forests and catch the view from its highest point.

~: ~

Brother Salvatore and I never made it to the shrine. We had to turn back about halfway in order to make it back in time for the after-noon office of None. Our slow pace and frequent stops kept us from reaching the top. As we walked back, the conversation wandered away from my research questions and into more personal and theo-logical topics. We descended past the Jesus statue once again, and I was reminded of how connected spiritual and physical work are for the monks of Guadalupe Abbey. Just as the lichen-encrusted arms of the statue were ever outstretched, this particular monastery for-est, nestled in the hills of western Oregon, invited all into its mossy embrace.

The Book of Creation

Catching me in the incense-laden hallway, his long, white cowl brushing the ground, Brother Berengar wanted to talk. He pulled me aside and spoke in hushed tones. He was in his fifties, muscular, with a shiny bald head crowned by brownish hair. His eyes peered out from a pair of thick-rimmed glasses. Berengar told me he had

had a very difficult time as a young monk. He struggled fiercely between his call to monasticism and the idea of pursuing a more active vocation as a parish priest. Taking his final vows at Guadalupe was ultimately a decision he made in the darkness of uncertainty. During the years leading to that final leap of faith, it was the land, the place, that buoyed him most in his anguished discernment and spiritual wrestling.

We moved into a small room overlooking the abbey cemetery and sat. Eagerly and without any prompting, he said, "Those years were very formative for me. My whole soul was really formed by the woods. Saint Bernard says, 'Beeches and oak trees surrounding Clairvaux have taught me more about God than any book.'"[78] Smiling, he opened his hands and said, "That was the experience I had." Working out his vocation—in Carlton, Oregon, of all places—Berengar invoked the memory of his spiritual forefather in Citeaux, France.

Saint Bernard, the boisterous twelfth-century Cistercian abbot who preached the Crusades, also spoke directly to the importance of place in forming the soul of the monk and echoed his spiritual elder Saint Anthony. When Anthony was asked what he did without any books, he remarked: "My book is the nature of created things; whenever I want to read the Word of God, it is always there before me."[79] The early European monk Evagrius Ponticus (345–399 CE) saw contemplation of nature, or *theoria physic*, as an integral part of the spiritual life.

The book of creation as a way of framing the monastic sense of place is deeply rooted in the *Logos*, the "Word" or divine principle of God found in the first chapter of the Gospel of John. Sixth-century theologian Maximus the Confessor (580–662) wrote that the Logos exists within each creature as a *Logoi*, a kind of spark, essence, or inscape at the center of creation's being.

Struggling with his vocation and reflecting on the impetus in the monastic tradition to become a "lover of the place," Brother Berengar began to pay more and more attention to the seasons and cycles of the place, and the land began to bleed into his experience of the liturgy, which he experienced as somewhat boring. He found again and again that time on the land soothed his restlessness, disappointment, and anxiety.

Sitting back in his chair, he continued, "I found that I would bring into choir my hikes, my experience in the woods. On a clear day seeing Mount Hood, or just discovering a new path. Seeing this time of year the trillium in bloom, or the wild iris, the daisies and wild roses." The changes in the liturgical cycles and in the seasons fused in ways that enriched his experience of both, just as they had for Brother Remigio of New Clairvaux.

On one occasion during Mass, watching the autumn leaves fall from tall maples from the windows of the abbey church, he realized that for the monk, "everything flows from liturgical life. I bring my life into the liturgy; my experiences with the woods, or when I was the gardener working in the soil watching things grow. My time alone in the woods helped me see what's being done here in the liturgy."

For Catholics, what is being done is the slow reconciliation of God and the world through Christ (the Logos).[80] The liturgy is the unfolding of the central events of the paschal mystery—birth, life, death, and resurrection—and just as the monks of New Clairvaux Abbey braided the agricultural and liturgical cycles, the monks of Our Lady of Guadalupe felt the ebb and flow of the seasons entangle with the steady spiraling wheel of the liturgy. The scriptures, liturgical books, and book of creation become volumes in an inseparable series that can be read and reread in any order.

∾ ∻

I asked Brother Berengar if working on the land had the same effect. He adjusted himself in his chair and pushed his glasses up the slope of his nose. He smiled with nostalgia and told me about his days on the forest crew under the tutelage of the wiry Brother Cluny, who served as the monastery's head forester for some thirty years. During his years on the forest crew, Brother Berengar was often assigned to planting trees and methodically weeding around the new saplings so they wouldn't be overtopped by grasses or blackberry. For Berengar, the act of planting trees was, in addition to its very practical purpose, a rich symbol of the spiritual life. What's more, it also provided a critical depth to a passage of spiritual writing given to Berengar by his abbot, days before he made his solemn vows. He was humbled by this experience, and as he related this story to me, he wore the emotion of it on his face as though it had happened yesterday.

"I worked in the woods," he said. "I would help with the planting of the seedlings in January and February, learning how not to 'J-root' the plants. My hand guiding it. That was a beautiful metaphor of the spiritual life—letting God guide us and being planted in deeper soil. There's a line from Jean Pierre de Caussade [1675–1751]. The abbot, before my solemn vows, knew that I was in a dark place. He knew I loved de Caussade; and he was reading from the *Abandonment to Divine Providence* just about three or four days before my solemn vows, and he found this line that he wrote and he said, 'I think these words will help you.' De Caussade says, it's like a prayer, '*You make the root beneath the soil flourish, and you can make fruitful this darkness in which you keep me.*'[81] So I put that in my pocket right here, and I have it, so it was over my heart as I was making my vows."

Scribed onto a piece of paper were words he kept close to his heart, and during his work on the land, he was writing "trees" into the book of creation. Writing that further connected him to the places where he walked and prayed, invoking not only the memories of the difficult work of tree planting but also the lessons written into the dark soil by the tree's chthonic roots.

〜 : 〜

As our conversation meandered, Brother Berengar and I shared our great affection for working with Brother Patrick and swapped stories about him that made us both laugh. "One experience I remember with Brother Patrick—we had to make a book run to Linfield College in McMinnville, and it was late afternoon. It was in December, and we were driving back at dusk. Before you turn into the driveway coming close to the turnoff, I could see the ridge, this ridge behind the abbey. And it was just palpable, it just spoke to me of God. You

know Gertrude Stein, when she went to Paris she said, 'There's a
there there.'[82] So, to me it was palpable, there was a silhouette up
against the sky, it was dusk, a winter day, and I'll never forget that. It
was just very consoling. Like, God's behind all of this. I'd seen that
ridge many times so you can't make it happen, so my experience of
God is that God hits you from the side, surprises you!"

God surprises you, even in a place with a thousand memories and
a mind full of theology and history. The book of creation is ever new.
It's not that the ridge was a symbol that pointed to God, but in that
particular moment there was an affective quality to the place that
was experienced rather than thought of. Like a familiar passage in
a poem, scripture, or novel, sometimes we can be struck with a sudden insight or epiphany. A merely symbolic reading of place renders
its features and meanings static, reproducible, and one-dimensional.
But as Berengar put it, openness to a place opens us to experiencing
it in new ways. As geographer David Seamon writes, "Encounter is
contextual—in different moments we experience environment differently."[83] Mood, disposition, weather, and season all conspire with
the ways place and landscape are encountered. The pages of the
book of creation are constantly being annotated through our experience of and participation with place.

Once, while Brother Berengar was at a silent retreat away from
Guadalupe Abbey, out walking, he was stopped in his tracks by a
particular tree. He leaned in a bit and, speaking softly, said to me,
"There was this Doug fir that had this gash, and there was sap drip-
ping out of it." He traced the contours of the gash in the air. "Immediately I thought of Christ—the blood and water flowing from his
side. I remember touching it, and it was a very holy moment for me.
My eyes were kind of opened to the experience of God. That God is
always with us. We're the ones who just don't always see it."

He paused and looked at me to make sure I was absorbing the
full import of his words. Almost as an aside, he added, "And then I
went back the next day, and it just wasn't the same."

The open gash in the tree became a glistening iconic symbol of
Christ's spear wound at the hand of a Roman soldier while he hung

dying on the cross. Berengar felt the mystical presence of God in that moment, but it was ephemeral, not repeatable. Though the memory of the experience is written in the pages of the place, it can only be invoked dimly.

∾: ∾

Standing together, Brother Berengar and I shook hands and walked out into the cool hallway. The smell of incense had faded, and the light pouring through the abbey hallway had begun to climb up the walls with the gloaming day. Work and prayer had formed the soul of Brother Berengar and written his own chapters into the book of creation. As one wise monk put it, however, there are also times when "charged moments" render a familiar place extraordinarily new. The book of creation is, in other words, a living, breathing agent in writing the story of its rich and evolving meanings.

A Hospital Visit

During my fieldwork at Our Lady of Guadalupe Abbey in 2016, Brother Patrick had a heart attack. He was in the hospital when I interviewed his brothers. Before I returned to Vancouver, I decided to visit him. I knocked on the hospital door and entered to see Patrick talking to a young nurse. He was covered with a thin blanket, and the wires and tubes of a heart monitor protruded from his open hospital gown. I sat down, and we talked about things at the monastery. He was waiting for his breakfast and asked if I wanted to do an interview. I told him I was just there to see him before I headed back to Vancouver, but he insisted, saying he didn't have anything better to do. So I went to my truck and got my recorder, and we talked for an hour or so about his long life as a worker and monk of the abbey.

Brother Patrick had been the master of work for Our Lady of Guadalupe Abbey for more years than he could remember, and he had developed a deep love for the place. He grew up on a farm outside Cleveland, Ohio, and joined the air force after graduating from high school. When he was discharged, he felt called to explore religious life. He eventually landed at Guadalupe a year or so after the monks had moved from New Mexico, thanks to a recommendation from a friend.

For Patrick, working the land was as integral to his spirituality as chanting the Psalms. When he arrived in Carlton, he was put to work on the farm as a lay brother, formerly called *conversi* under the feudal system. This meant he lived a totally separate life from the "choir religious," as he called them, who were mostly priests. He never wanted to be a priest; it was farmwork that drew him to monastic life. In his slow, soft manner, he related how he came to the monastic life.

Folding his hands over his chest, he began, "Well, one of the reasons was, like I say, farming. I liked farming, and it was a contemplative life, you know. We didn't have schools or parishes. And the brothers themselves impressed me very much, very much. As a matter of fact, that was almost the main thing, the simplicity of the place and the people themselves." Back then, the entire farm was run by the lay brothers. They woke up early, ate a simple breakfast of bread and coffee, and said a short liturgy of the hours out in the fields.

The monastery bottomlands were planted to grain, and they grazed sheep and cattle on the pastures and uplands; Patrick was at the heart of it. He loved the work and was particularly fond of raising sheep. Cracking a sheepish smile, he said, "I had a sheep that used to follow me around like a dog. Yes, it was a ewe that had twins and one of them died, and so I took care of the lamb and bathed it and took care of it and then it used to follow me all around the barn."

Chuckling a little, he continued, "Some of the brothers used to tease me about that, but it was the cutest little thing. I enjoyed it."

When a small pack of feral dogs got into the herd, the monks had to shoot several of them because they were maiming the sheep. Patrick said that was one of the few times he got really angry, and I could see that the memory still affected him.

The decades leading up to and immediately following World War II saw a significant rise in monastic vocations across many orders. Brother Patrick was one of many young Roman Catholic men drawn to monastic life during that time. With an abundance of young men, typically trained in some kind of trade, monasteries were bustling farm-churches and, for the most part, self-reliant.

Unfortunately, almost simultaneously with the rise in monastic vocations and new monastery foundations in North America came the restructuring of the U.S. agricultural economy, which phased out price supports for direct commodity subsidies. This restructuring had a dramatic impact on monastic work. With relatively small properties compared to commercial farming operations, many monasteries simply could not keep their farming operations profitable or even self-sustaining. Some Benedictine monasteries concentrated on their other apostolates, such as running colleges or seminaries.[84]

The more contemplative monasteries like Guadalupe Abbey often decided to lease their farmland and transition to more manufacturing-based income generating activities, rather than sell their lands. Leasing land ensured that it would not be developed, maintained a buffer of solitude, and brought in a modest income. Our Lady of Guadalupe was forced to close its farm in the early 1960s and transitioned to its current suite of income-generating activities: book binding, fruitcakes, and a wine storage and labeling facility.

When Guadalupe's farm went under, some of the brothers left the abbey in protest. Brother Patrick was saddened but determined to stay. "I didn't give it a second thought, because I had taken a vow of obedience," he said. He knew he was supposed to be there, and he found plenty of other meaningful work to do.

A big change came in 1969 when, during a general chapter meeting of the Trappist order, they decided to fully integrate the lay brothers with the so-called choir monks, who until then had formed a kind of religious caste system within each monastery. Rooted in the medieval *conversi* system, lay brothers ran much of the farming on the Cistercian monastery's extensive holdings. This decision was made in recognition that lay brothers had become a kind of second-class citizen-monk, but certainly the shift in agricultural policy tilted the scales. Patrick complained that when Gua-

dalupe Abbey integrated and he was given a black-and-white habit
that had until then been reserved for choir monks, "it was not very
good for working in, because it would get dirty too fast." We both
chuckled at this.

~: ~

A nurse brought in an orange cafeteria tray with orange juice, plas-
tic cutlery, and a steaming plate of pancakes. Brother Patrick sat up
with a grimace and began to slather butter on his pancakes.

"Patrick," I said, "are you sure you want to eat all that butter?"

He looked down at his plate and thought for a moment, and then
looked up at me. "Yes," he said, with a laugh.

Patrick weathered the changes to monastic work with grace, and
after the farm closed, one of his favorite jobs was clearing and re-
building the walking paths and trails that crisscrossed the extensive
property. During my first stay at the abbey in 2014, Patrick and I
worked on a section of trail that had washed out in the rain. Gathering after the office of Terce, we would say a short prayer in his
cluttered office and head to the backhoe. We loaded the bucket
with tools, gravel, fence posts, and metal piping. Patrick drove, and
I bounced and lumbered along the gravel monastery roads coughing
from the bursts of thick diesel smoke that belched from the wheeled
lumbering beast.

To restore the trail, we needed to dig into the bank a few feet
and then put down gravel along a section of trail. We worked slowly
but steadily and eventually brought the trail up above the mud. We
then installed a railing along one of the steeper sections by pound-
ing metal stakes into the bank and using metal clamps to attach a
length of salvaged metal piping as a handrail. It was good work, and
the four-hour intervals before we headed back for lunch were just
enough to make me feel like I had accomplished something without
being too tired. Brother Patrick was eighty-four, and he still worked
hard. Sometimes he had to stop and catch his breath as he pushed
the wheelbarrow up the hill to get more gravel. He would turn to
me and smile, shaking his head, regretting that he didn't have the

energy he used to. I was secretly glad he didn't, as some of the monks had discreetly admitted to me that when they were going through formation many years ago, Patrick had been a bit of a taskmaster and they left work totally exhausted. They also spoke fondly of their time with him, and those who still worked with him always looked forward to their time together.

Brother Patrick was a simple man with a simple theology. He finished his pancakes and opened a small orange juice with shaky hands with IVs protruding from paper-thin skin crossed with small rivers of blue veins. I asked him why farming harmonized so well with the monastic life.

"Well, it's being close to earth, for one thing," he said, "and nature itself, just working around the trees and the brush and animals. I think it's a wonderful thing because I actually think God almost made us that way. Everybody, well not everybody, a lot of people, I would say, like their solitude and silence. And working with nature really brings you closer to God. I like to think that one of the main purposes of going to a monastery is to try to get closer to God, and that's one way I think you can do it, through nature."

Working the land and being in nature put Patrick in contact with God's presence; for him, each creature was a window into the heart of God. Scratching his head as if to stimulate a thought that was forming, Patrick got a little philosophical:

Where does this come from? Who made this? Is this all natural stuff? It makes you think, at least it does me, anyway. I see a big old redwood tree, and I could just stand there all day and look at the crazy thing! How could anything be so big? The size of the seeds of those crazy things is so small, it's unbelievable! It's just wonderful, just wonderful. The organization of the world itself, almost everything just slips into place. We have our storms and our hurricanes and tides and all this wild stuff, but it's so well organized. I just feel closer to God when I get to nature, when I'm working with animals and the ground.

As one monk said of Brother Patrick, he was a true Trappist.

For Patrick, the world itself was the best argument for the existence of God. Work was therefore not only a prayer but a means of experiencing God through the place Patrick called home. Farming and working the land felt like cooperating with God's creative energies in making the land more productive and beautiful. Patrick's vocation as a farmer-monk was inseparable from his work among the fields and forests of the Oregon hill country that had been his home for more than sixty years.

~: :~

I really enjoyed working with Brother Patrick during my visits to Guadalupe Abbey. Our talk in the hospital in 2016 was unfortunately the last time I ever saw him. He died on April 23, 2017, while he was mowing the guest house lawn. I wasn't surprised to hear that he died doing what he loved—working. When I returned to the monastery in early 2017, the monks were restoring and clearing much of the trail along the swale that had become overgrown since Patrick's death as a way to preserve and honor his legacy, which had been written into the very ground of the abbey's extensive trail system.

Alone with the Alone

CHRIST IN THE DESERT ABBEY

I'm so nothing, I'm so everything.
RABBI ABRAHAM HESCHEL

Brother Ubertino held his black scapular to one side so he could scramble up a cluster of boulders. He had brought me to one of his favorite spots. We stood before a rocky outcropping just north of Christ in the Desert monastery's cloister, deep within the Chama River Canyon Wilderness. It was a clear day in late April, though flurries of spring snow had been threatening all week. Like their monastic forefathers, the monks of Christ in the Desert find their remote desert canyon—accessible only by a single thirteen-mile dirt road—an ideal place to live out their vocation of work and prayer.

I joined Brother Ubertino on a ledge, and our conversation fell into admiration for the surrounding cliffs. I asked about the stories of *brujos*, or evil witches, near Owl Rock, and the circumstances of an experienced hiker who I heard had tragically fallen from one of the nearby ledges to his death. Brother Ubertino shared his deep love for the Psalms and how he could not help but think of their imagery as he walked along the river's meander or the footpaths at the base of the canyon walls. Like many of his fellow monks, his memories and life experiences echoed and ricocheted off the colorful deep-time strata exposed in the cliff faces of the Rio Chama Canyon. His maturing as a monk was in constant dialogue with this canyon, and the symbols of monastic spiritualty had become an indispensable key to reading the land.

~: ~

Two monks out for a walk in the vast high desert of New Mexico

Christ in the Desert Abbey was founded by three monks from
Mount Saviour Monastery in upstate New York in 1964, inspired
by the spirit of the Second Vatican Council to rediscover the roots
of their monastic order. The founders felt called into a deeper observance of monastic silence and wanted to find a place that was more
remote—wilder than what New York had to offer. Father Aelred
Wall, a monk of Mount Saviour, began to scour the western United
States for the right place. Eventually he found what was then a remote cattle ranch in northern New Mexico.[85]

The property is located on the banks of the Rio Chama. The
closest village is Abiquiu, thirty miles southeast, home of the Geor-
gia O'Keeffe House Museum, one of the former residences of the
twentieth-century painter. The area is considered high desert at
7,500 feet, and the vast, open view-scapes are pixelated by pinyon
pines and junipers and shaggy carpets of dark green conifers at the
higher elevations. The Rio Chama Valley is somewhat lush and supports a rich diversity of wildlife, from mountain lion, black bear, and
mule deer to beaver, colorful migratory birds, and coyote.

The adobe chapel at Christ in the Desert Abbey blends into its surroundings

When I visited in 2016, the monastery was a bustling community of more than thirty monks, half of whom were under fifty. The monastery began with 115 acres on the west bank of the Rio Chama, but when a property across the river became available in 1978, the monks quickly raised the funds to purchase it, bringing the total acreage to 275 and preventing a potential encroachment on their solitude.

The abbey's stunning adobe chapel was designed by architect George Nakashima and completed in 1968. From a distance, the chapel feels like a natural feature of the canyon ecology with its rustic cross and earth-toned walls.

Due in part to the community's remoteness but also to its strong commitment to ecological sustainability, the abbey has been a champion of green building since its founding. The monastery's structures are all built from adobe, wood, and stone. When it was expanded in the 1990s, straw bale construction was used, and the monastery was the first private property in New Mexico to install solar panels. The abbey received the Renew America Green Building and Real Estate Development award in 1998.

The area is the traditional territory of the diverse Pueblo peoples, who have inhabited New Mexico's canyons and mesas and the surrounding high deserts from time immemorial. The ancestors of today's Pueblo peoples built the elaborate cliff dwellings of Mesa Verde and developed a sophisticated astronomy at Chaco Canyon. In many places they grew maize on the mesas with a form of dry farming. The Spanish conquest incorporated the Rio Chama Canyon into the Spanish land grant system.[86] When the United States took over after the Mexican-American War ended in 1848, many Indigenous and mestizo Mexicans lost their family or communal lands to Anglo settlers. In 1915 huge chunks of the area were annexed by the U.S. Forest Service during the establishment of Franklin D. Roosevelt's forest reserve program, headed by conservationist Gifford Pinchot. In the 1960s a surge of Chicano and Indohispano activism led by Reies Tijerina (1926–2015) sought the return of some of these lands. In 1996 Tijerina and several activists visited the monastery to locate the ruins of the abandoned village of San Joaquín.[87]

∾ː∾

After a comfortable silence, I asked Brother Ubertino if he thought this place was sacred. The Latin root for the word is *sacrare*. In its conventional sense, sacred means to set apart, usually for religious purposes, and refers to the sacred groves and temple precincts dedicated to the gods and goddesses of the Greek and Roman pantheons. A place was sacred when it was associated with the deeds or consecrated to the veneration of a particular deity like Zeus, Apollo, Dionysus, Aphrodite, or Artemis.

Brother Ubertino sat for a while and then drew out the question, testing his assumptions against his instinct to say yes. "My hesitation is this," he said, rubbing his short salt-and-pepper beard. "A church is four walls, and it is four walls where we human beings set aside a space to worship God. Thus it becomes sacred."

"Okay," I said. "Simple enough."

"One foot outside of the church, is that sacred? Well it could be, but is it less so? Anything set apart for God alone, that has the greatest sacral character, and so a church is a sacred place, it's a refuge, it's sanctuary—*sanctus*, you know, holy."

He paused and then began again. "We can take holy things and make them unholy. I'm sure plutonium has good uses because it exists, and God created everything. There's not a destructive drug among them, but it's the *way* we use them. Clearly, land has been put to abysmal use, and land has been put to holy use. So is the land sacred? It's nuanced."

In Roman religion the *genius loci*, or "spirit of the place," was venerated, consulted, or at the very least revered as an unquestioned reality. Collective associations built shrines or temples to these spirits, and with the rise of the Roman emperors in the early years before the Christian era, the *genius* became the protective spirit of the entire Roman Empire.[88] This enchanted quality of the land was a widespread assumption in virtually all pre-Christian European pagans, where local gods and goddesses were associated with specific places or ecologies such as the sky, springs, wells, mountains, groves, the sea, or caves. The *sense* of these places, however, was not always affection or fondness and could just as easily be foreboding and fear.[89]

Brother Ubertino was hesitant to commit to the unequivocal sacredness of places because for him, and many Catholics, sacredness denotes the quality of a relationship, not a characteristic of the world, which for him is understood as being a creation of God, who alone is holy. Christianity has, it seems, held God and the places of the world in tension.[90] The heresy of pantheism, in which God is assumed to be the same as or coterminous with the world, has always been a thorn in the side of theologians who wish to keep God and the world at a distance. It has also been a primary threat from those earthy mystics and poets who see the spark of the God they worship at the heart of all things.

A more nuanced understanding of God's relationship to the world is through the lens of *panentheism*. This theology does not deny God's ultimate transcendence (otherness) but tends to emphasize God's immanence (within-ness) in the world. Another way to say this is that panentheism is the belief that the world is in God and God is in the world. Because God is understood not as *a* being, but as Being itself, the world is sustained at every moment by God. When the apostle Paul was preaching to the Greeks at the Areopagus in Athens, he said, "For in Him we live and move and have our being" (Acts 17:28).

For many Christians, a sacred place does not encapsulate God's presence but points to and participates in it. Just as many of the monks I spoke with understood the world to be a kind of icon of God, a panentheistic theology affirms that the Creator is perceptible through the creation. This has sometimes been referred to as a "sacramental" or "incarnational" approach because it emphasizes God's immanence in the world. For example, the poet Gerard Manley Hopkins (1844–1889), a Jesuit priest, wrote in his poem "God's Grandeur" that "the world is charged with the grandeur of God."[91] Hopkins's beautiful poetry frequently invokes this sacramental immanence—God's indwelling presence at the heart of all creation, molten in its singular mystic inscape.

Thomas Merton developed this idea in his essay "Everything That Is, Is Holy," where he beautifully describes the intricacies of his own sense of monastic place at his monastery in Kentucky:

> The form and individual characters of living and growing things, of inanimate beings, of animals and flowers and all nature, constitute their holiness in the sight of God. Their inscape is their sanctity.... The special clumsy beauty of this particular colt on this April day in this field under these clouds is a holiness consecrated to God by His own creative wisdom and it declares the glory of God. This leaf has its own texture and its own pattern of veins and its own holy shape, and the bass and trout hiding in the deep pools of the river are canonized by their beauty and their strength. The lakes hidden among the hills are saints, and the sea too is a saint who praises God without interruption in her majestic dance. The great, gashed, half-naked mountain is another of God's saints. There is no other like him. He is alone in his own character; nothing else in the world ever did or ever will imitate God in quite the same way. That is his sanctity.[92]

Merton's attentive awareness to the particularities of place recognizes the minute intricacies of a leaf, the unique pattern of a horse's coat, or the etchings of erosion written into a nearby mountain as expressions of God's presence and creative energies experienced through and read from creation.

In her landmark but controversial work *The Body of God: An Ecological Theology* (1993), theologian Sallie McFague (1933–2019) defends an even more immanent view of sacredness, writing, "Radicalizing the incarnation, therefore, by using the model of the universe as God's body is neither idolatry nor pantheism: the world, creation, is not identified or confused with God. Yet it is the place where God is present to us. Christianity's most distinctive belief is that divine reality is always mediated through the world."[93] This sacramental theology insists that the world is and has always been the *place* of God's revelation to us. This view pushes beyond the conventional interpretation of the Incarnation being a union of the divine and human natures exclusively in the person of Jesus of Nazareth. But McFague does not suggest that the doctrine of the Incarnation upheld as a unique event is the same as holding an incarnational view of creation, which simply affirms that God is present to the world though never wholly circumscribed by it. This tension is what Brother Ubertino was wrestling with as we sat in a place that radiated the sacredness of creation but was not in a strict sense a consecrated religious space.

By way of contrast, in her book *India: A Sacred Geography* (2011), Diana Eck documents the dizzying diversity of India's sacred places. She illustrates their diverse and sometimes contradictory stories and their deep significance to Indian religious and spiritual life. Many devotees go on pilgrimage to these sacred sites, and temples are often built atop areas of particular sacredness, such as the reputed site of the birth of Krishna or the defeat of Ravana by Ram. The Ganges River is experienced *as* a goddess, and bathing in her waters is a means of ritual purification.[94] The river is sacred in its own right, not just through any sacramental connection to the transcendent Brahman. In addition, there may be as many as a hundred thousand sacred groves in India, each devoted to any number of local deities who have their own personalities, taboos, and requisite appeasements.[95] These groves are sacred because they are understood as the abodes of these fierce and generous gods.

Of course, Catholics have their share of sacred objects, sacramentals, relics, and sanctuaries. For most Catholics, however, a place is not sacred in the same way as it might have been for a Roman pagan or in the way it is for an Indian Adivasi or devotee of Shiva.

Theologian of place Belden Lane suggests that one of the most important axioms for understanding a Christian engagement with place as sacred is that "sacred place is not chosen, it chooses."[96] These charged moments, as one monk called them, which attach to places, suggest that sacredness is not fixed but can break through when it is least expected. As Brother Berengar of Guadalupe Abbey shared about his trip with Brother Patrick to McMinnville, experiences of distinct sacredness are often surprises. Catholic sacramentals such as scapulars, rosaries, icons, and holy water are charged with sacredness, but it is often ordinary places, ordinary times, or passing between places that mark themselves as memorably sacred, inscribing themselves into a monk's moral landscape and sense of place.

~: ~

After a bit more chatter and a few jokes, as we neared the end of our conversation on the ledge, Brother Ubertino and I again fell silent in the face of the towering canyons to our front and back. We rose, dusted ourselves off, and began making our way back to the cloister. The chiming bells echoed through the canyons, calling us back to the *axis mundi* of the chapel and to the Opus Dei of the Liturgy of the Hours. For Ubertino, the views in this canyon spoke of the grandeur of God and whispered of God's presence. But so too did the walk from cell to chapel in the murky dark of morning, the flicker of a candle before an icon, or the laughter of a fellow monk. Places do not have to be particularly impressive to be sacred. As Belden Lane writes, "Sacred place is ordinary place, ritually made extraordinary."[97]

All Dogs Go to Heaven

Brother Sillan has a Franciscan heart and a deep love for animals. An energetic Latino with short hair and dark stubble for a beard, he was comfortable and kind from the first moment we met and treated me like a dear friend. He spent most of his time in the massive monastic garden kindly bossing young novices around in a melodic mix of Spanish and English. I spent the afternoon shaping garden beds as he repaired several stone terraces. The weather was once again threatening, and dark clouds loomed low in the sky. At one point a cloudburst of hail let loose and we had to seek shelter in the toolshed. I started to feel skeptical that a garden was a good idea in this place.

During one of many breaks, we sat on some tree stump stools and chatted as we drank from bottles of water. Seemingly out of nowhere a small flock of geese flew overhead just feet from our heads. We cried out in surprise and watched as they glided onto the muddy water of the Rio Chama. "Beautiful," Sillan muttered.

Wrapping up our break, we got back to work. Like the other monks, he had come to Christ in the Desert for the beauty and deep silence of the place. He had lived a very different life in a major city on the West Coast, and he said one day he just left it all behind. Sillan felt that he was a bit of a radical among the monks because he had a strong affinity for animals and plants. He ate a vegan diet, whereas most of the rest were pescatarians and ate dairy products. He made a huge fuss if any of the monks killed a rattlesnake, and he tried not to kill bugs or worms with his tools when he was gardening. Laughing a bit at himself, he said, "You have to treat animals with respect. They are your brothers!"

Then, mimicking an imaginary interlocutor with a sour face, he pantomimed, "No, they are not my brothers!"

Turning and pointing, he retorted, "Yes, they are your brothers!"

He looked over at me, stood, and patted his hands at his sides in exasperation. "Who made you?" he said. "God. Who made them?

God. Oh! Same Father? Brothers!" He began laughing a hearty got-cha sort of laugh.

"They are kindred," he continued. "They can feel love, attachment, they can suffer! Have you ever seen a pig cry? Tears running. And have you seen a cow in terror? A dog suffering with a broken leg? Hmm? Or a dog really being himself with sheer joy? It's part of us, it is part of God! It's part of feeling. I don't dare say it's a collective soul, but they're sentient beings!"

Skirting around the dreaded language of pantheism, I assumed this meant he did *not* believe animals had souls. I stood up and, with hands clasped around the top my hoe, said, "But no soul?"

"Yes! I think they are, yes! There will be some traditionalists who will say, 'Oh no, they are creatures,'" he said, with his mimicking face. "Of course, there is no 'dog-ma' on the question of animal souls!" He erupted with a laugh.

For the Greek philosopher Plato, whose assumptions about the natural world are evident in Catholic theologians like Thomas Aquinas, plants and animals had vegetal and animal souls, just not *rational* souls like humans. After the European Enlightenment, however, the stark dualistic philosophy of René Descartes fostered a view of animals that saw them as so much raw material destined solely for human use, with no intrinsic value.

The Catholic Church has not mused much over the years on the topic of animal souls. Even in *Laudato Si': Care for Our Common Home*, Pope Francis's 2015 encyclical letter, he does not make any such claims, although it is a passionate piece of ecological theology. In it Francis outlines the major ecological problems of climate change, pollution, and biodiversity loss. He decries a civilization obsessed with convenience and technology that conditions us to see the world and its creatures as exploitable and disposable. He preaches an *integral* ecology that does not fetishize wild nature but seeks to better care for all of earth's marginalized creatures, human or not. And he takes a bold step toward recognizing that animals are not just objects for human use but beloved creations of God. Speaking of ecosystems, he writes, "We take these systems into account not only to determine how best to use them, but also because they have an *intrinsic* value independent of their usefulness. Each organism, as a creature of God, is good and admirable in itself; the same is true of the harmonious ensemble of organisms existing in a defined space and functioning as a system."[98] Francis stops short of proclaiming that all dogs go to heaven, but he gets pretty close.

∾ ∶ ∾

Brother Sillan was old school. He certainly affirmed the Catholic teaching that humans were made in the image and likeness of God, but his Franciscan heart saw all of creation as kin, and he had imbibed *Laudato Si'* during his early morning study time since the day it was released. Suddenly, turning from his work on the terrace, Sillan looked at me with excitement. "I have a really cute story!" he said.

"Do tell," I said.

"Well, I had this dog. She was three years old when I got her. She was my friend for ten years, and we hiked together and everything. She was my companion. We even shared the same room and everything. I let her sleep on my bed, and sometimes I would sleep on the floor. We just treated each other as equals. And when Silvia died something very interesting happened that convinced me more of the animal soul. I knew she was passing, and so I held her. She looked at me, and all that I could see was that she was going to leave. Hanging in my window, inside my cell, I have this mobile made of clay that is so heavy that of course it's never going to move. I mean a hurricane could come through the window, and those clay things hanging there are never going to move. When Silvia died, those things started spinning, and then bling! bling! bling! bling! making sounds like a bell. I looked up and I knew it was her. I just looked at her and sensed that she left this body. I felt this kind of like joyful energy." Sillan looked down, perhaps feeling a bit vulnerable about relating a memory so close to his heart.

"That's a beautiful story," I said, smiling. "I'm convinced." We held each other's gaze for a second and then continued working the red sand that passes for soil in the high desert of New Mexico.

Not Quite Canterbury Tales

There are many tensions embedded in Christian theology—between immanence and transcendence, place and placelessness, word and silence. Brother Venantius embodied his own set of tensions with charm. He was a contemplative with something of a temper. He was a monk that looked and acted more like a cowboy.

I joined him under the shade of a cottonwood tree while hummingbirds chirped and jockeyed with each other in the crowded airspace around a small bird feeder. Venantius had come to Christ in the Desert from a different order, and when he arrived a deep sense of peace came over him that felt like home. He spoke with a bit of a gruff twang but had a sparkle in his eye that put me at ease.

He loved to talk about politics, and more than a few times we went down rabbit holes that left us far from my intended talking points. On his skepticism toward the environmental movement, he pontificated, "We need an environmental movement of the soul! Because we pump all this porn all over the place, and everybody wants to drink spring water. You want to dip your body in polyurethane so you can have sex with anything that moves, but you go to Whole Foods, because God forbid somebody put a chemical on your tomato!" For Venantius, environmentalists were too often concerned with the minutiae of controlling environmental problems while completely ignoring moral ones. I couldn't say I agreed, but his analogy made for a hilarious image.

Brother Venantius had a talent for preaching and teaching. He used powerful analogies and images. When he talked about the meaning of the Passover sacrifice, I felt like we had been transported back to Jerusalem, and I could almost smell the smoke of the grapevine prunings being burned in preparation for the feast.

While describing the doctrine of the Incarnation, wherein God took human form in the person of Jesus of Nazareth, he gestured wildly with his hands, saying, "God reached into the far end of the universe, like grabbing the back end of a balloon, and pulled it back the other direction. He's made himself present by becoming part of the created order precisely so he can pull the entire created order into himself."

Venantius also helped me see the mechanics of charged moments, times when sacredness breaks through into particular places, in a different light. With the spunk of a Baptist preacher, he barked, "I can't create it. The Lord makes himself present, as he makes himself present. Since I'm inside God right now, the inflow of the ocean into my soul happens at his discretion, not mine! If it happens at his discretion while I'm reading scripture, or while I'm in Eucharistic adoration, or praying the Rosary, magnificent; if it happens while I'm walking alone, or sitting, or watching the river, magnificent; his choice! I'm not so foolish as to think my reading of scripture or my walking alone, or looking at this particular mountain, is what did it, so that I've got to get back here tomorrow at four o'clock to watch God come back into my soul again. It's not that way, you're not in charge."

For Venantius, God is not a place-based vending machine the monks strive to insert their consciousness into at will, expecting a uniform or standard experience of presence or sacredness. Even participating in the Eucharist or praying the Rosary aids in achieving a measure of inner stillness, but they do not *produce* God's presence. Silence may be God's habitat, but that habitat is not a zoo. For monks, the presence of God is a wild creature, and what better place to catch a glimpse of God than in the wilderness?

~: ~

Our conversation meandered like the nearby Rio Chama. One of the threads that most intrigued me was the time we spent discussing the nature and evolution of monasteries as retreat centers where people often go to experience some kind of authentic monastic spirituality. A tension has arisen between the desire of some monks to return their monasteries to greater agricultural self-sufficiency and follow the Rule of Saint Benedict more closely by working with their hands, and the expectations of the many urban dwellers who come to the desert for solace, reflection, and the quiet beauty of the abbey's natural landscape.

Despite the romance of the rule, the property is not ideal for farming or even gardening. The soil is sandy and infertile, and the property is located between two very tall canyon walls that shade the valley floor in the morning and late afternoon. The weather is often unpredictable, and flurries of snow often push into early summer, constantly threatening frosts. But as we have seen, the spiritual life and the liturgy are enriched by the practice of farming and manual labor, and those who are in touch with the rhythms of farming seem to be better able to understand and experience the world of the Bible, the symbolism of the Psalms, and the rich spiritual lessons of place.

I asked Venantius about the pros and cons of having a more self-sufficient monastery and whether there wasn't some measure of romanticism in seeking this out. Leaning back in his chair, he smirked a bit. It seemed I had touched on something he had wanted to get off his chest for a while.

"Look," he said, "the retreatants want Canterbury Tales! 'I'd like to come and see Canterbury Tales!'" Eyes widening, he sat up. "And they think we grow our own food, and we have our own garden and the monks are out there. It's all so"—he paused to find the right word—"authentic!" he said, pointing at me as he found it.

"I just sit there and go, no, in order to make this work I've got to be riding a combine ten hours a day, and you're not going to want to sit and read your book with me out in the field working a major farm! And again, I don't blame them, it's a gorgeous setting, and if they come out to the most remote monastery in the Western Hemisphere, Christ in the Desert, they've come out to be remote and they've come out to be quiet."

Pausing and putting his face in his hand, he muttered, "And then they want to participate in the work and work alongside monks and chat and all that kind of good stuff. And they'd like to be doing some agricultural work, but again we're talking about fifty- or sixty-year-old retreatants. Because they're not all in their twenties! Those are the people that are all out making money, earning a living! People that have a disposable income come out and stay in one of our guest rooms and they want to *participate*." He hung his head between his knees and chuckled.

Looking up again he said, "So I got a fifty- or sixty-year-old lady who wants to come out and pull some weeds. That's who I got! I'm not going to get forty men coming out here who are all in their thirties and they want to bust ass for three weeks and pull in my crop!"

Brother Venantius suddenly became aware that he had revved up a bit too much. He sat forward, lowered his voice, and interlaced his fingers in a kind of prayerful posture.

"Listen, we do the hop harvest every year. We're going to harvest the hops. Okay, so I'm assigned ten monks to help harvest the hops. The librarian, eighty-four years old, he's almost blind."

He unclasped his hands and, pointing at nothing in particular, raised his voice and said, "I mean, I get the guys who have nothing else to do, and then I get a couple of guests who are interested and they are usually here for two days and then they bag!"

He put his hands on his thighs, calmed down, and continued, "They want to just pick the hops by hand, and chat, and talk about God. Lady! I got three freaking rows I've got to get in today between now and 12:30 when everybody quits, move it! Pull the dang things off the dang vine and move it! Which they don't, so I do it, but now I'm sitting there going, okay, why am I so ripping ticked?"

I began to laugh softly, trying to keep my composure. Taking a breath, Brother Venantius started laughing too. He shook his head and finally stood defiantly and yelled, "I'm ripping ticked because we've got this nonsense agricultural presence and I'm doing all the work by myself! I get one other guy and I can do more in two hours than I can get ten guests to do in four!" He collapsed into his chair and we both roared with laughter.

~: ~

Brother Venantius is a good monk. His frustrations were often off the cuff. I include them here not to embarrass or lampoon him but to illustrate an important tension that exists in many contemporary monastic communities. A monastery is meant to be a self-contained unit of contemplative prayer, yet while vocations have declined, the number of those interested in retreats has surged. Each of the monasteries I visited struggled to balance their need for contemplative solitude and silence with the ministry of the place, which draws hundreds if not thousands of visitors, retreatants, and pilgrims to these places each year. Christ in the Desert Abbey has always been known for its strict adherence to the Rule of Benedict, and as the community evolves, I have no doubt that they will navigate this tension with grace.

Silence Incarnate

I was waiting for Brother Malachi on the porch of Christ in the Desert Abbey's bookstore after Mass on a bright spring day. I could see all the way across the Rio Chama to the steep, rusty canyons on the other side. The sheer vastness of the view turned my gaze upward toward the sky, and it seemed to open my chest and lengthen my posture. The air was still, and even after having been at the monastery for a few weeks, I marveled at the place.

Hopping up the steps with a smile, Malachi shook my hand. He was of slender build, clean-shaven with a small black monastic cap on his shorn head. We decided to walk down to the river and explore the muddy banks. He wore his all-black habit and kept his hands tucked behind the thin scapular that draped down the front and back. The river gurgled softly as we walked under the shade of cottonwood and willow trees. He was shy at first, but we were soon in the thick of a lively discussion. We discussed American Catholicism, nature writing, and the importance of silence.

We sat on logs under the shade of some willow trees. Malachi removed his black knitted cap to scratch his shaved head. He twirled his scapular slightly, looking at the ground. He was very much committed to what he called "wilderness monasticism" and had tried living at several different monasteries before committing to Christ in the Desert. In hindsight, he suggested that each one was slightly more remote—from a suburb in Massachusetts to a rural area of

Oklahoma, and finally here. He had been sure he wanted to be a monk, but the place where he would live the rest of his life was the final, crucial part of that decision.

Though I noticed he was not great with his local flora identification, dwelling in the wilderness had taught Malachi that the natural world was an icon of God. Turning his face upward toward the sun, which was veiled in a thin gossamer of cloud, he practically chanted, "God is the reason why everything around us still exists. From the most complicated city down to the simplest ant that's crawling in the grass somewhere. Since God is upholding nature in being at every moment, there is an invitation in nature to see the divine reality that is making all of this possible from moment to moment. So it follows that the contemplation of God is preceded by the contemplation of nature."

As I learned from Brother Ubertino, nothing could wholly contain God, but the being of each creature pointed to God as the source of Being. This awareness was, of course, accessible in other places, but for Malachi it is more readily apparent in this wild place. Intuitively pointing south toward Santa Fe, he sneered and said, "There's nothing about a mall or a parking lot that predisposes us to have a contemplative experience of God. But there's something about a wilderness setting that, if we let it, will, like this river, just sort of carry us into a spiritual moment." Wilderness monasticism for Brother Malachi was a covenant to witness God at the heart of *this* canyon, day in and day out.

Another important feature of wilderness monasticism for Malachi was the natural silence the Rio Chama Canyon afforded. Taking a small sprig of willow in his hand as we began walking again, Malachi twirled it in his fingers and then softly grabbed it with his other hand. We were quiet for a moment and then, flowing naturally with his own stream of ideas, he applied this to his community.

"You can think about the Rule of Saint Benedict being incarnate in a certain place versus another place," he said. It is true, it is the same rule, but each community embodies, or *incarnates* in his words, the rule differently. And for that matter, each monastery therefore incarnates silence differently. After braving the dust-and-mud adventure they call a road that turns off the main highway, the first thing I noticed when I arrived at Christ in the Desert was nothing. I stood outside the guest house almost aghast at the quality of silence.

There is a theology here. While institutional churches tend to emphasize the correct wording of creeds, theology, canon law, and what constitutes a sacrament, the desert hermits (not rejecting any of the above) immersed themselves in the silence of their wilderness retreats. Silence was experienced as a conduit of God's living presence. In his book *The Blue Sapphire of the Mind*, Douglas Christie writes, "The Word speaks through the world and it is necessary to learn this language. But there is also the rich ground of silence in which the contemplative listens, the physical silence of solitude and the interior condition of *hesychia* or stillness in which the Word can be apprehended and absorbed."[99]

This distinct way of approaching God has given rise to differentiating between the complementary *cataphatic* and *apophatic* forms of theology. In its cataphatic mode, practitioners embrace the particularities of words, language, symbols, and metaphors about the divine. In the apophatic mode, they tend to move through, with, or beyond these symbols toward contemplative silence. For example, Dionysius the Areopagite, who many early Christians believed to have been converted by Saint Paul in the Areopagus, sought God in the "brilliant darkness of a hidden silence" or, as another translation puts it, "the dazzling obscurity of the secret silence."[100] For many contemplatives, silence acknowledges that God is ultimately ungraspable, beyond our words about God and outside of human comprehension. The spiritual practice of saying the Liturgy of the Hours is punctuated by and culminates in silence.[101] As theologian J. P. Williams writes, "To speak about a God who is beyond all concepts, words, and definitions we need a language that will unsay itself."[102] That language is silence.

For Malachi, wild places and their incarnate silence are conduits of the divine. Both their symbols and their silences speak. The intensely personal spiritual experiences of the monks were not something to boast about. I perceived hints and whispers that many of the monks regularly sink into that territory beyond time and space and into the unified whole that they call God. Underneath every symbolic landscape of speech lay a bedrock of silence and between each word a blessed hush.

॰: ॰

It took a while, but eventually even Brother Malachi and I ran out of things to say. We planted ourselves on some logs and watched the Rio Chama calmly chortle through the silent canyon as the abbey bell began to clang and echo off the canyon walls.

Silence before the Mystery

Brother Berach whistled and called, "Rosie! Joshua!" It was the loudest I had heard a monk talk in my months of fieldwork. He was worried about his two small dogs, one of which was quite new to the abbey and hadn't learned to avoid rattlesnakes. Being late spring, he was hopeful that they were not yet active. But his concerned hollers punctuated our fruitful discussion.

I liked Brother Berach. His was the last interview I did during my visits to these four holy places. He is a jolly sort, unfiltered in his polemical honesty about other monastic orders, extreme environmentalists, and especially the dread secular humanist. He has southwestern Indigenous heritage, his mannerisms are confident, and he is quick to laugh and self-deprecate.

We made our way out of the cloister garden where an acacia tree was buzzing with honeybees. Brother Berach used a walking stick, and his light-colored hiking shoes looked a little odd sticking out from under his black habit. We found our way to a trail running parallel to the Rio Chama, but we could not see it or hear the river's flow. Trees and scrub lined the trail, and the towering canyons preached from both sides. We spent several minutes talking about the community and the growth it had seen in recent years, rare for a contemporary monastic community. Having been there from nearly the beginning, he was proud of the community the monks had built in the wilderness. He loved the life of a monk, and he loved the liturgy, but his love of the power of silence was even more profound.

Discussing the Psalms, as I did with most of the monks, he quite naturally connected them with the land. He reflected, "When I'm out walking, you know, I'm reciting the Psalms. I look at the trees. The images from the Psalms come to mind, and I begin to think about them."

He began chanting a line from Psalm 1, saying, "'He's like a tree near running water!' Say, we've got that!" he joked. "What does that mean? Well, I have it there to look at, you know, and I have the images graven in my mind because I've memorized them, and I repeat them every day. You can't understand the Psalms unless you begin to understand the land! And you can't really understand the land as God's creation unless you begin with the Psalms, see?" He smiled. I nodded.

The rich pastoral and poetic imagery of the Psalms acts like a template through which monks see the world. The symbolic world of the Bible is a key with which Brother Berach interprets the features and seasons of his homeplace. However, each monastery, each place incarnates, as Brother Malachi said, the Psalms differently, so that the Psalms, which are everywhere the same, come to life in the place in different ways. The symbols of the Psalms conspire (literally breathe) with the land, and a monk's sense of place is never solely symbolic, made up only of static signifiers and signifieds, but always embodied, lively, dynamic. The Psalms interpret the place, and the place interprets the Psalms.

Brother Berach's musings about the Psalms' embodied qualities reminded me of a story related by another monk of Christ in the Desert. He was on a long hike when it began to snow. He turned back but soon had lost his way. He started to fear he might die. When he finally made his way back to a recognizable trail and found his way home, he immediately thought of Psalm 111:10, which says, "The fear of the Lord is the beginning of wisdom." "That psalm took on a whole different meaning for me and a whole different depth," he told me. "When I say that psalm now, I immediately connect with that experience I had out there in the wilderness." The symbol of fear was embodied in the experience of being lost, and the psalm and the experience are now indistinguishably fused within the monk's sense of place.

For all his love of the place and the Psalms, however, Brother Berach had something of an apophatic streak. Playfully frustrated with our increasingly cerebral theological discussion of place, he shook his head and said, "There has to be a point where we're just in silence before God and also in silence before the beauty that he's created without trying to put things on it, see! Letting go of all that imagery and being here in the presence." A symbolic landscape or a psalm leads one into contemplation. That is what the practice of Lectio Divina is meant to do. Once a passage of scripture has been read, meditated upon, and prayed with, contemplation is meant to move through but beyond the word into silence.

Berach waved his hands toward the canyon and looked back at me briefly to make sure I was following. I nodded. He smiled and, in a hushed tone said, "That's what I think contemplative life is supposed to be about, learning to be in silence before mystery and nothing further."

Apophatic theology also cautions against framing the world in only positive, uplifting terms. Silence can be toxic just as it can be nourishing. Wrestling with the sacredness of creation, most of the monks emphasized the cataphatic mode, the ways creation points to or participates with God. Malachi and Berach spoke to me of silence, but only one monk I spoke with during my fieldwork ever spoke of the experience of the absence of God. Walking with Berach, listening to his profound theology of the Psalms and of silence, I recalled my conversation with Brother Jorge of Guadalupe Abbey. Speaking of his deep love for the woods of Oregon, he said, "Sometimes I feel the absence of God in creation. God is not creation. Because if you look at creation, creation is also cruel. There's war, the trees are fighting each other, are killing each other for air and space and light, so creation is sometimes what the poet says, 'red in tooth and claw.'

"I sometimes I go for a walk in nature, and I get this terrible, empty feeling. It's a really empty feeling, and I feel nature say to me, 'Don't look for your beloved here, we are not your beloved.' And when you read the mystical theology of the church, from Origen to Gregory the Great and Saint Bernard, you find that mystical theology of the bridegroom that says our soul is made for God. Saint Augustine has it too: 'Our souls are made for God, and they are restless until they rest in him.'

"So, there's a part of us that nothing in creation can fill. There's nothing that will. We are made to see God, and God is not a creation, he's a Creator. So creation reminds me, it says, 'Yes, we're beautiful and you can enjoy us, but don't forget who you really are and who you're really made for.' And sometimes it reminds me very, very starkly. I go for a walk in the winter, and everything is cold and dark and damp, and I just feel the emptiness, the absence of God completely. But that absence can be a very, very good thing. It is a spiritual experience in itself." Presence needs absence, cataphatic needs apophatic, immanence needs transcendence, word needs silence.

It was not until a few years after my interview with Brother Berach and Brother Jorge that I understood what he meant. At the time, it seemed like he was simply cautioning me against a facile pantheism, as most of the monks oft were wont to do. Don't get too comfortable with creation, make sure to leave room for transcendence and silence before the mystery. But during a midwinter hike near Bellingham, Washington, I experienced something of this foreboding absence. It was getting near dark, and as I picked up the pace to ensure I made it back to my car, I felt an overwhelming sense of dread, darkness, and gloom and remembered Brother Jorge's words. In Saint Augustine's wording, being made for God means there will always be something of a longing for transcendence in our lives, even if we are privileged enough to sink deep roots into place or experience the beauty of wild nature. Even for Pope Francis while articulating a profound ecological theology in *Laudato Si'*, he cautions against what he calls the "stifling immanence" of a narrow pantheistic environmentalism.[103] This is why

Brother Berach wanted to teach me that much of the contemplative life can be summed up in silence before the mystery. To fetishize nature, place, a church, or a monastic habit is to risk idolatry and hence to never fully embrace our true nature as human beings. The monastic tradition, with its deep roots in the deserts of the Middle East, teaches that silence is the best kind of teacher and the likeliest habitat of the divine.

◌⁚◌

As we made our way back to the monastery, Berach wandered into a polemic against the dangers of secular humanism and the slippery slope of euthanasia. We stopped near his office, and I thanked him for his time, letting him know that his was my last interview and I would be leaving in the early morning. He blessed me and prayed over me and wished me well. I smiled, touched by his kindness and a little disoriented by how quickly he could move from polemicist to pastor. His two dogs nipped and spun, and I reached down to pat their dusty, burr-speckled backs.

I turned and walked through the monastery cloister and into the vast expanse of the Rio Chama Valley. Clouds overhead traced shadows on the hallowed ground, and the sun shone in undulating waves on the ancient canyon walls that sat stoic in their grandeur. The scene crackled with a verdant aliveness that could only be called grace. I breathed the desert air as gravel crunched beneath my feet and walked in silence back to my lodging to pack and gather myself before the long drive home.

Wrestling with God on the Rio Chama

Sunset was near. I had mostly packed and was ready to depart in the morning. I found a beautiful bend in the Rio Chama about a mile from Christ in the Desert Abbey to watch my last day of fieldwork pass into silence. Four monasteries and more than fifty interviews in less than four months. I was tired, but a well of gratitude was swelling in my heart.

The moon rises over the tranquil Rio Chama

A mostly full moon peeked her face over the eastern yellow mesas to watch as the sun set beyond the red mesas to the west. I knelt and squished some fine clay between my fingers from the tea-with-cream-colored banks of the river. The waters whispered rumors of summer, and the buds of willow and cottonwood and scrub oak whispered back. I stood and shook my hands, my fingers throbbing with the bite of the icy water.

Suddenly a dozen or so tree swallows appeared and began to flit and warble around me like the water that eternally caresses the un-seen stones of the riverbed. They darted upstream and then worked their way back down again. I was mesmerized. It felt like the kind of charged moment I had heard the monks speak about. The energy of the birds seemed to pulse and sputter through my body, and I felt layers of anxiety and self-doubt release into the chocolate river.

I remembered an interview I had done a few days before. As we wrapped up our discussion, almost as an aside, the monk recalled a story about two Tibetan monks who had visited the monastery a few years back. They loved the community so much that they stayed for more than two months. "They fit right in," he said.

During a conversation, one of the Tibetan monks asked what the river was called that ran through the monastery. "Chama," the brother had said, which he explained was a Spanish pronunciation for *Tzama*, which means a place of contest or wrestling in one of the Puebloan languages. He told them that he had heard that the river's eastern confluence had been a center for Puebloan competitions and games before Europeans arrived. The Buddhist monks nodded and said that in the Tibetan language Chama (which they must have heard as some pronunciation of Tara) was the name for the Goddess of Mercy. The monk looked at me, smiled, and paused. "So," he said, "mercy flows through the monastery."

Jacob wrestled with a heavenly messenger on the banks of the Jabbok River and became Israel—one who wrestles with God. There is mercy in wrestling, I thought. Throughout my time as a researcher, it had certainly felt that way. Each monastic community welcomed me with open arms, and I had learned so much. Each place—the Carthusian monastery in Slovenia, the California coast, the Central Valley of California, the foothills of western Oregon, and the high desert of New Mexico—had felt in its own way like home. And as I prepared to wrap up my field season, flashes of treasured places, conversations, and quiet moments of insight flickered before my mind.

Throughout, I have tried to illustrate the contours of the monastic sense of place. I have shown that ancient values, beliefs, traditions, and symbols serve as a template through which the landscape is interpreted and read. This rich meaning is culturally constructed—monks *learn* the theologies, doctrines, spiritualities, symbols, and histories of their tradition and interpret their places and experiences with them. There is a deeply symbolic or iconic sense to their understanding of the world as pointing to God through the particularities of the places they call home.

Crucially, however, monks also seek to become lovers of the place, sinking them into a profoundly *dwelt-in* reality. This means that sense of place is also shaped by embodied experiences that emerge from and through the day-to-day habits of living in place. Monks engage in daily liturgical prayer, wandering, and work. This engagement attaches memory, meaning, and lesson to the locales and seasons of the monastic landscape, forging the varied senses of place and spiritual ecologies I have attempted to illustrate.

The monastic sense of place is indeed deeply rooted, yet paradoxically it is also consistently rootless, emphatically affirming the goodness of creation while looking through and ultimately beyond creation to the Creator. Transcendence and even absence are as fundamental as the sense of immanence and presence. Over a lifetime, monks nurture a deep dialogue between inner and outer worlds, between the inscape of their souls and the landscape of their places. Silence is an essential container for this rootless rootedness, this emplaced placelessness.

My time with the monks has taught me that to dwell in the wilderness is to explore the depths of the human heart and the mystery at the heart of the world. But it is also to believe that though we make many heartbreaking mistakes, human beings have a place within this fragile earth community. We must do better.

As the swallows began to disperse, day surrendered to twilight and the moon rose into full pale brightness over the deep peace of the rugged canyon, and I turned and walked back toward the monastery. While very few of us may become monks in the coming years, it is my hope that we might all be willing to wrestle with the difficulties of a changing climate in our places and by so doing prepare ourselves to journey through the dark night ahead.

Monastic Wisdom
for the Anthropocene

In the night of our technological barbarism,
monks must be as trees which exist silently in the
dark and by their vital presence purify the air.

THOMAS MERTON

In his 1959 novel *A Canticle for Leibowitz*, science fiction writer Walter M. Miller Jr. explores the cyclical nature of history through a
postapocalyptic future set in a Cistercian-style monastery. The first
of three parts opens on a novice named Brother Francis preparing
for his vows by taking a retreat amid the civilizational rubble of the
Utah desert. Global civilization has been debilitated by nuclear war,
and Francis's monastery has dedicated itself to preserving literary
and technological memorabilia from before the so-called "Flame
Deluge." This is necessary because, after the deluge, a backlash
against technology resulted in the Age of Simplification. There was
widespread pride in illiteracy, and mobs of self-proclaimed Simple-
tons organized regular book burnings.

Francis's order had been founded by Isaac Edward Leibowitz, a
Jewish electrical engineer who worked for the U.S. military. Leibowitz took refuge in a Cistercian monastery after the Flame Deluge
and later took vows when his wife was presumed dead. Leibowitz
dedicated the rest of his life to "booklegging," as it was called—preserving human knowledge by saving books and information from
being destroyed. His fellow monks founded the Albertian Order of
Leibowitz to focus on this important task.

The novel illuminates the recurring amnesia of human civilization, especially the thread of human culture that gets caught in the

cycle of technological advancement, absolutist power, and the ne-
glect of spirituality. The author does not anticipate the present day
in which climate change or species extinction are at the fore, but the
last paragraph of the novel closes with a single shark that, Miller
writes, "was very hungry that season," swimming deep into the sea
to escape the fallout of yet another civilization-destroying nuclear
war that had driven a select few pioneering monks of the Albertian
Order into space. The shark drifts into the depths while a remnant
of humanity is forced to survive away from the very planet that gave
them life.

Implicit in the novel is the historical period wherein medieval
monasticism was instrumental in preserving human knowledge
during the so-called dark ages of Europe. After the Flame Deluge, monasticism serves a similar purpose, yet ultimately one that
undermines humanity's ability to remain on earth because of the
consistent pattern of abuse of industrial technology in the service
of power, greed, and warfare. While the threat of nuclear war is still
with us, the deep anxieties about its imminent eruption have more
or less been backgrounded by the metastatic advance of species extinction and climate change. As a result, the planet is in flux, and
while change is the only constant in the earth's history, the evidence
is overwhelming that human beings are the primary actors behind
many of the destructive changes being witnessed across the globe.
Perhaps the monastic sense of place can provide yet another sanctuary during what many are calling the Anthropocene.

In recent years, the term *Anthropocene* has caught on as a way of
describing the rise of human influence on the biological and climatic
patterns of earth. Atmospheric chemist Paul Crutzen defines the
Anthropocene as "an informal geologic chronological term for the
proposed epoch that began when human activities had a significant
global impact on the Earth's ecosystems."[104] This new era is proposed
to be different from the Holocene, which presented a more or less
stable climate within which human civilization evolved.

Humanity has been on a steady resource-intensifying trajectory
since our domestication of fire, and this trajectory jumped with the

invention of agriculture and again during the industrial revolution. Some have suggested that the Anthropocene inadequately captures the root of what is ostensibly an industrial cause. Yet, since its inception, it has caught on and is the springboard for talking about our current era, even by proposing alternatives such as the Capitalocene.[105] Climate change is going to impact various places differently, so it seems to me that witnessing and attending to our places should become one of many tools in our toolbox of responses to the current crises.

Conversatio Morum

The central monastic vow of *stabilitas* or stability can motivate a deep sense of place. The monk enters the monastery to seek God and, in seeking God, finds himself accompanied by habits, fears, anxieties, and those of his companions. The monk's path means choosing to live in one particular place, and to wrestle with God nowhere else. The monastic has committed to become more and more with and for the place as a means of sanctification. Like Siddhartha Gautama, who resolved to sit under the fig tree until he reached enlightenment, monks sink deep roots into place so their branches will grow tall and strong toward the sun of divine light.

Another vow monks make is *conversatio morum*, literally the changing or conversion of one's manners (mores) or habits over a lifetime. By vowing to engage in *conversatio morum*, monks commit themselves to a lifelong engagement with cultivating virtue and holiness and conversion to the ways of God. Interestingly, *conversatio* can also be translated as conversation. *Conversatio morum* then could also be interpreted as committing to having a lifelong moral conversation with the world.

Many of us are engaged in conversations about how to change our lifestyles, how to reduce our carbon footprints, and how to effect structural and global change at a scale that will make a difference. These are crucial areas of activism. But engaging in a *conversatio morum* with one's place is also, as the Western Apache taught Keith

Basso in *Wisdom Sits in Places*, a way of letting our places *teach us* how to live with them. As we have seen, monks develop intimate bonds with place that involve symbol, memory, experience, and lesson. Sense of place is not a one-way road but a conversation between people and place.

Over the millennia, monastic wisdom has abided in the shadows of our bustling civilization. A monastery is a sanctuary, not only for the souls who come to call it home but for those of us who need to take refuge from chaotic lives devoted to progress and productivity. Monastics generously and without fanfare whisper to the world: slow down, stop a minute, pay attention, listen, pray, give thanks, take a walk in the woods. At the dawn of the so-called Anthropocene, where there are many visions competing for how best to address multiple ecological crises and criticism of the importance of place in addressing the crisis, monasticism offers a powerful example worth emulating. And while monasticism will perhaps never be the social and political force it once was during its medieval golden era, and monastic communities are microscopic as a share of the global land base, monastics will continue to quietly offer their wisdom to the culture like yeast to bread. They invite us to engage in a *conversatio morum* with our places so that we might be better able to discern what the most effective ways forward might be.

A Liturgy of Place

In addition to issuing us this challenge to engage in deeper listening, the monastic sense of place invites us to attune to the unfolding liturgy of our places. In Nan Shepherd's book *The Living Mountain: A Celebration of the Cairngorm Mountains of Scotland* (1977), we read a rich description of the Cairngorm Mountains, an experience of place that is embodied and engaged. "Place and a mind may interpenetrate till the nature of both is altered," Shepherd writes. "I cannot tell what this movement is except by recounting it."[106] Her aimless wanderings in the mountains of Scotland further illustrate what I have attempted to describe here. Encounter and charged moments may be found, not just by the cloistered few, but by anyone who is willing to pay attention to how body and land enfold each other in the ongoing liturgy of place. This liturgy of place has been amply illustrated, but here are a few gestures toward getting it out of the monasteries and into our everyday lives.

A Lectio of the Land

Lectio Divina is the monastic practice of slow, contemplative reading of scripture, often the Gospels. While the liturgy is filled with scriptural readings and symbols, in the early hours of the morning, often between Vigils and Lauds, most monks will sit in a quiet place and immerse themselves in scripture as an act not of scholarly comprehension, or even the extraction of truth, but as a reverent imbibing of the words of Jesus.

A *lectio* of the land calls for engaging in a deeper reading of the book of creation and of the ways our places help write their own stories. To attempt over a lifetime to read the landscape is to understand that the world is not simply what we make of it, that the world speaks to us as well, and that most of the world's mysteries are beyond words. To become literate to place means that we turn our attention toward the cycles, seasons, and varieties of life in a given place. This is the lifelong practice of learning the names, habits, and seasons of the flora, fungi, and fauna that our places share with us.

In her book *Braiding Sweetgrass* (2013), Robin Wall Kimmerer, a member of the Citizen Potawatomi Tribe, struggles to learn her Native language and reconnect with her people's traditional lifeways. For Kimmerer, listening to plants and animals is not a metaphor but a practical necessity, and to love the earth is to acknowledge and admit that the earth is capable of loving us back.[107] For those of us rooted in the Abrahamic faiths, the boisterous praise of creation in the Psalms provides a resonant voice with Kimmerer's vision and the many, many others who are attempting to shift global consciousness toward a recognition of the earth's sacredness and our connection to all the living beings with whom we share this breathing planet.

We must learn to read the signs of changing seasons, learn to meditate on the intricate patterning of leaves, pray with the calls of birds, or grieve the flailing bodies of spent, dying salmon. And then, always, we come to rest in the silence of the place, the unsayablenesses, the suffering, the absence, and the uncertainty of the coming days.

Wildness All Around

In *Dwelling in the Wilderness*, I have shown that while some monks make their homes in the wilderness (New Camaldoli Hermitage and Christ in the Desert), for many others the most daunting wilderness to be faced is that which we find within the human heart.

The tension between wilderness and paradise is discernible throughout the Bible as an extended motif for Israel's longing to be in right relationship with God. Enlisted by early monks, wilderness was both the spiritual ecology of silence and a powerful analogy for the garden where God awaits the monk in the wilds of the soul.

For those of us with the privilege, time, and skill, hiking and backpacking in North America's wilderness areas can be a powerfully moving experience, where we encounter beauty, wildlife, and our own limits. But wilderness is as much an idea as an ecological reality. Under the influence of this understanding, it can seem like our connection to place or our spirituality of nature can only start once we cross a park boundary or get onto the trail.

In William Cronon's controversial 1995 essay "The Trouble with Wilderness; or, Getting Back to the Wrong Nature," this idea of wilderness takes a hit. Cronon tells the story of wilderness not just as an institution that sets aside nature in its wild state but as an idea. Wilderness in the West has come to mean that domain of reality *separate* from human culture.

To be clear, a liturgy of place is not against wilderness. In an era of voracious capitalist expansion, I am nothing but grateful for the early conservationists who worked tirelessly to preserve places like the Mariposa Grove, Redwoods National Park, Yellowstone, the Grand Tetons, Banff National Park, and the Adirondacks, among many other early protected areas. Yet the notion that the natural world is

best managed as a place without any human presence led some conservationists to hold unconscionable views toward Indigenous peoples. John Muir, for example, the founder of the Sierra Club, spoke
with contempt of Indigenous peoples and celebrated their being
forced out of their homeplaces to create Yosemite National Park.

Cronon accuses conservationists and preservationists of preaching a dogmatic standard of wilderness as pristine. He is not against
preserving wild places but sees the broader conservation movement
articulating an ethic that not only contributed to the forced removal
of Indigenous land stewards from their traditional territories but
also came to value wilderness areas over and above *any* place that
had been modified or "tainted" by humans.

Ironically, the landscapes most valued as wilderness by nature
writers such as Henry David Thoreau and John Muir were far from
it. Thoreau's cabin was located in a second-growth forest on Ralph
Waldo Emerson's property. What's more, it was only a mile or so
from the village of Concord. Muir's Yosemite Valley had been stewarded by the Ahwahnechee people for thousands of years through
annual burning that gave the valley its open parklike structure.
When Muir described it, he compared it to the Garden of Eden.
For Indigenous peoples I have read and learned from, whose ancestors have tended the land for many thousands of years, the purity of
an untouched place carries precisely no meaning at all. It is not that
Indigenous peoples have been perfect ecologists, but that as Nuu-
chah-nulth land steward Gisele Maria Martin has quipped, "We
don't have a word for 'wilderness' in Nuu-chah-nulth languages....
The closest translation is 'home.'"[108] Dwelling in the wilderness is to
say that wildness and home are not mutually exclusive.

Cronon also argues that the pristine "wilderness ethic" has led to
the mismanagement of the very wilderness areas it values so highly.
For example, for most of the twentieth century, fire suppression was
the official policy of North American conservationists and resource
managers alike. The idea was to let nature take its course without
any destructive interventions, human or not. To intervene in a
wilderness area was to taint it with our human footprint and thus

despoil its purity. This fire policy came into serious question in 1988 when more than three thousand square kilometers of forest burned in Yellowstone National Park. While climate change is unequivocally a factor in the rise in wildfire severity and acreage, a legacy of hands-off wilderness management is also an important factor, especially in fire-adapted areas of the North American west.

This well-intended but misguided wilderness ethic has led many of us to devalue or ignore the places we could have the deepest connections to—homeplaces, neighborhood ponds, commons, groves of trees, gardens, farms, and hedgerows. Not denying that there is a rich spirituality to be felt in wild places, Cronon writes, "when I think of the times I myself have come closest to experiencing what I might call the sacred in nature, I often find myself remembering wild places much closer to home."[109] His critique of pristine wilderness as a gold standard of environmentalism has not resulted in a movement to declassify our wildlands but rather has encouraged conservationists to also value places on the margins. Ecological restoration initiatives, expanding city parks and green spaces, establishing community gardens, suburban bird watching, urban forestry, and even reinhabiting cemeteries as social spaces are ways that many of us might more deeply engage with landscape and place. In the essay's powerful final words, Cronon writes, "If wildness can stop being (just) out there and start being (also) in here, if it can start being as humane as it is natural, then perhaps we can get on with the unending task of struggling to live rightly in the world—not just in the garden, not just in the wilderness, but in the home that encompasses them both."[110]

While the wilderness movement has often emphasized the power and beauty of our most grandiose places, we must recognize that in addition to these icons of beauty and the sublime, the wildness of ordinary things also deserves our awe. Dwelling in the wilderness is not just about finding picturesque landscapes or distant deserts and old-growth forests; it is also about paying attention to the particulars of a place, the ways our own senses and body respond to the ordinary and the unexpected. These are ways of inscribing our memories, stories, and even life lessons into the places we traverse most. We do not always need to travel long distances to connect with wildness; it is often on display in our bodies, backyards, and neighborhoods. Wildness is all around, and we do not need to wait for the weekend drive to the national park to experience it.

Going beyond Words

To learn the names of things is to engage with the particularities of the world. Yet a fastidious attention to details can lead us to miss the big picture or, worse, to reduce the world to a sum of its parts. A liturgy of place, a *lectio* of the land, an attunement to wildness, should also make ample space for silence and stillness, for awe, wonder, and mystery. In some spiritual circles, the desire to commune with nature invokes the place as a doorway to the divine. Feelings of peace or serenity come to be expected while walking in the cool of a summer day. A leaf, tree, or pine cone becomes a moral lesson on perseverance or resilience. And while attending to place encompasses all these possible encounters, as theologian Belden Lane wisely warns us, "the challenge is to honor the thing itself, as well as the thing as metaphor. When Emerson declared in 1836 that 'every natural fact is a symbol of some spiritual fact,' he sent people racing to the woods, anticipating the voice of God in the call of every thrush. But too often they paid scant attention to the songbird in their anxiousness to hear some transcendent message. They returned home full of nothing but themselves, their pockets stuffed with metaphors."[111]

Lane is pushing our sense of place from the cataphatic toward apophatic—the need to sometimes go beyond words, metaphors, images, and symbols into silence. Theologically speaking, cataphatic prayer is filled with liturgy, symbol, and aesthetic beauty. But while God is aimed at with words, ultimately God is beyond those words, and apophatic spirituality rests in the silent mystery that is at the heart of God.

For some, perhaps those who long for communion with the places themselves rather than any notion of God, going beyond words is an invitation to see ourselves as fundamentally rooted in the natural world. Ursula Goodenough's "Religious Naturalism," for example, does not appeal to any metaphysical framework for a sense of the sacredness of the world. For her, the mystery and complexity of being is wonderful enough.[112] Writer Sara Maitland's *A Book of Silence* (2008) resonates with this more pantheistic approach. In the book, which also explores the depth of the Christian tradition on silence, Maitland attempts to capture in words an unexpected charged moment she had while living in Scotland:

> I sat on a rock and ate cheese sandwiches—and thought I was
> *perfectly* happy. It was so huge. And so wild and so empty and so
> free. And there, quite suddenly and unexpectedly, I slipped a gear, or
> something like that. There was not me and the landscape, but a kind
> of oneness: a connection as though my skin had been blown off.
> More than that—as though the molecules and atoms I am made of
> had reunited themselves with the molecules and atoms that the rest
> of the world is made of. I felt absolutely connected to everything.[113]

Maitland's experience of mystical communion with her place was felt as a kind of oneness with everything around her. While the monks I met never claimed to dissolve into the landscape, those with a stronger pantheist bent may find this passage more resonant with their own spirituality of place. Maitland's experience was not chosen; it chose her, and it was not in any particularly exotic, far-off wilderness but near the place she was living. Her experiences show us that we can learn quite a lot about the particularities of the world but can never fully know the world in its entirety. Going beyond words means reserving a space in our liturgy of place for reverence, aimless wandering, unexpectedly charged moments, stillness, and ample silence.

Despite my penchant for analysis and theory, my love for learning the names of plants, mushrooms, constellations, or geological strata, there are times when I put my ID apps away and just sit and watch the light of the setting sun dance through the shaggy canopy of a beloved forest. As landscape writer Robert Macfarlane writes, sometimes the only word we need is "wow!"[114]

Place-Holding

Australian philosopher Glenn Albrecht thinks a lot about place, both locally and globally. He is worried that as the so-called Anthropocene spreads, some places are becoming less and less recognizable to their inhabitants, Indigenous and otherwise. Albrecht is not opposed to change. In his book *Earth Emotions* (2019), for example, he begins by zooming out to the farthest reaches of the evolving cosmos, writing, "The universe is a place of restless and endless motion."[115]

Yet while change may be a constant, not all change is created equal. After being raised on Australia's remote west coast, Albrecht eventually pursued a doctoral degree in Newcastle. He became an avid birder and began exploring the Upper Hunter Valley in New South Wales, falling in love with the place. For Albrecht, each of us can come in contact with a deep, even primordial sense of place no matter where we live. Our emotions around place can manifest as either positive or negative—positive when our bond to place is strong, negative when that bond is threatened or violated.

Inspired by E. O. Wilson's idea of biophilia, defined as "the urge to affiliate with other forms of life,"[116] Albrecht had a proudly transformative experience on one of his birding trips. He was overwhelmed by the impact of the contrast he felt between the beauty of the Hunter Valley and an open-pit coal mine he stumbled across in the uplands. Albrecht began searching for a way of talking about and describing the feelings that come up when one is confronted with the radical changes to place that are all too common in the dawning Anthropocene.

Albrecht sensed that it was something akin to nostalgia, from the Greek *nostos*, place, and *algia*, meaning pain or discomfort. He first coined the term *place-algia*, but he admitted that the word doesn't exactly roll off the tongue. He eventually landed on a combination of the Latin verb *solari* with *algia*, and coined the neologism *solastalgia*, or comfort-pain, to capture the feeling of anxiety that destructive change to one's homeplace can cause. Since he coined the term in the early 2000s, his concept has caught on in various venues that are

concerned with theorizing and responding to the Anthropocene. Albrecht more fully defines the word as "the pain or distress caused by
the ongoing loss of solace and the sense of desolation connected to
the present state of one's home and territory. It is the existential and
lived experience of negative environmental change, manifest as an
attack on one's sense of place."[117] Not the secular techno-functional
placelessness that defined modernity, which Albert Camus called a
kind of "nostalgia without aim," but the feeling of a change to the
places we know and love.

The experience of solastalgia can manifest as both a strong reaction to the changes affecting a specific place or as a generalized
anxiety about the state of global change, which is being discussed
using the mental health terminology of climate anxiety. Robert
Macfarlane has praised the concept even as he laments its necessity:
"Solastalgia speaks of a modern uncanny, in which a familiar place is
rendered unrecognizable by climate change or corporate action: the
home becomes suddenly unhomely around its inhabitants."[118]

Solastalgia is not just a clever neologism for stewing urbanites. It
has been documented in communities where extractive industries or
climate change are affecting traditional hunting, gathering, and land-
care practices. Among Inuit communities in circumpolar regions,
which are warming at a much faster rate than the mid-latitudes, climate change has impacted their traditional sense of place in light of
shifting patterns of weather. These changes are directly reflected in
their sense of well-being. Activities such as hunting, fishing, forag-
ing, trapping, and traveling have been impacted by these changes—
changes that have subsequently impacted not only physical but also
mental, spiritual, and emotional health and well-being.[119] From
receding glaciers and the shifting ranges of culturally important
species to mountain top removal in Appalachia and sea level rise in
Alaska, the Anthropocene promises many more negative changes to
the places we call home.

Despite the daunting challenges ahead, Albrecht affirms the
call to work toward what he calls the Symbiocene, a world where
mutually beneficial human-earth relations come to replace our pre-

dominantly commodity-based and extractive relationship to places. Philosopher Donna Haraway has used this phrase in her work, and in the 1980s theologian Thomas Berry similarly called for the dawn of the Ecozoic Era.[120]

Place-holding, then, seeks to name and work through difficult emotions with respect to the negative changes to our places. It is also a commitment to stay with our places even when things seem impossible. In Douglas Christie's estimation, commitment to place is the commitment "to struggle with the way both place and loss of place shape and form us."[121] Attuning ourselves to our places is not simply the cultivation of a romantic affection for our places but a determination to witness and resist their willful destruction and a willingness to let our hearts break with holy grief when, at last, they are.

Places that have been modified, damaged, or degraded by human activities can still be deeply loved. Trebbe Johnson, a wilderness guide and author of *Radical Joy for Hard Times: Finding Meaning and Making Beauty in Earth's Broken Places* (2018), calls on us to bear witness to wounded places. Each year her eponymous organization holds "Earth Exchanges" where people gather in wounded places to make offerings or create art, dance, and beauty.[122] The hope is that these acts of love will not only serve to reinhabit marginalized or shunned places but will also heal them both spiritually and ecologically. In our attempts to defend, protect, and restore our places, we must be willing to hold them and be present to the changes that affect them, willing to both celebrate victories and grieve losses.

Against Place

Sense of place is not a panacea for the world's problems. It is not one single thing. It is, more than anything, a posture of openness to what the place offers, come what may. It is important therefore to highlight some of the criticisms leveled at sense of place from various corners of the ecological humanities literature. There are legitimate cautions to place that see it as a kind of privileged localism, especially among wealthy communities. Agrarian writer Wendell Berry, for example, who has written extensively about the value and importance of place, has also received criticism for a vision of place that privileges the rural. His fictional characters in novels such as *Jayber Crow*, for example, seem to long for a kind of imaginary simplicity and backward-looking nostalgia for times gone by that ignore the painful stains of racism and Indigenous genocide that have been all too pervasive in North America.[123]

Social scientists Carolyn R. Schaffer and Kristin Anundsen, writing about the challenges of building community, note that a strong and insular localism has historically risked devolving into parochial xenophobia.

> As tightly knit and stable as most old-style communities were, they were also homogeneous, suspicious of outsiders, socially and economically stratified, emotionally stifling, and limited in opportunities for personal and professional development. So long as members belonged to the right ethnic, religious, or racial groups— or stayed in their place if they did not—and behaved within a narrowly defined set of parameters, they could count on strong communal support. But if they strayed too far outside, their fellow community members might well shun or harass them.[124]

A commitment to place can sometimes look more like a boundary marker than a welcome mat. For example, the conflict between Israel and Palestine often resorts to a kind of spiritual autochthony that has taken advantage of global geopolitics to weaponize ethnic and religious identities to control the narrative of who truly "belongs" to that place.

In India, Hindu nationalism has weaponized many sacred sites in its rhetoric against the Muslim minority. For example, the Babri Masjid is a mosque that was built during the Moghul rule of the subcontinent in the sixteenth-century atop the sacred site of the god Ram's birth. In 1992 a Hindu nationalist mob tore down the structure, and in recent years the Supreme Court has sided with the act as a legitimate restoration of a Hindu sacred place.[125]

Literary critic Timothy Morton balks at the potential romanticism of place-based approaches that would, for example, take issue with a proposed wind farm because it would spoil a favored view. An illusory wholeness hides the planetary impacts done by the coal power plants that are far from the community and the impact across the globe of extracting the coal that is burned in those plants. The wind farm may be visually disruptive, but it is arguably better for the global climate crisis than continuing to burn fossil fuels. Morton laments that we tend to prefer "secret pipes, running under an apparently undisturbed landscape" to the more obvious wind turbines with their lower-impact carbon emissions.[126] This "not in my backyard" or NIMBY-ist instinct is a serious caution against seeing place as a kind of country club whose primary purpose is for our mental well-being or leisure rather than the whole of our lives and livelihoods, and the global community of places.

Australian ecofeminist philosopher Val Plumwood (1939–2008) cautions against an overemphasis on place in light of global economic homogenization. "The very concept of a singular homeplace or 'our place' is problematized by the dissociation and dematerialization that permeate the global economy and culture," she writes.[127] By this she means that in an era of increasing globalization, attachment to place in the industrialized and developed nations often comes at the expense of other places that are ecologically sacrificed on the altar of global market forces to support our Western lifestyle. Unfortunately, attachment to place all too often ignores the impact we have on locales that are out of sight and out of mind.

A very different but nonetheless fascinating critique of place comes from scholar of religion and ecology Whitney Bauman. He agrees with Plumwood that the romantic drive in Western culture to "go back" to authentic places loses its meaning in an economy that is quickly stripping the planet's places of its resources. "Much of ecological and religious thinking is tied up in securing home, community, place, identity, value, and meaning," he writes. "This is juxtaposed with the globalized postworlds in which we live, where such stability, arrival, and homecoming is not possible, nor perhaps even desirable."[128] For Bauman, sense of place has mostly meant a kind of wishful thinking that seeks to arrive at a stable and secure existence, rather than an ecological strategy for responding to global crises. Like Plumwood, he argues that romantic notions of place such as wilderness or pristine nature, could in fact be perpetuating the ecological crisis by hiding the impact of our lifestyles in faraway places while we insist on protecting nature closer to home.

Interestingly, Bauman's proposal by analogy is that rather than a "monogamous" approach to place, we would be better served in the Anthropocene by a move toward what he calls a "nomadic polyamory" of place, which would decenter our beliefs about authentic sense of place being rooted in a singular locale. He argues that patriarchal culture has sought to dominate people and planet, and contemporary ideas about place as a form of monogamy reproduce these patterns of abuse in their own way.

I find important truths in all these cautions; however, I am not sufficiently convinced by these critiques to believe we should abandon place-based approaches to ecological problems. The monks in this study certainly adhere to both a deep sense of loyalty to place and a blatantly romantic notion of the world as a sacramental reality that reveals the peace and goodness at the heart of God. Yet their romanticism is not a fantasy; it is a deeply committed relationship that has wedded them to a place and to a community.

First, monastic solitude is not a misanthropic or escapist isolation. A monastery is meant to be a sanctuary *for* the world *from* the world, albeit on its own terms. While monks are called to pray, they are not praying just for themselves but for the world as a whole. There has been and always will be in monastic spiritualty a wider awareness to the world and deep commitment to hospitality, to welcoming the world to the places they call home. Their rootedness gives them the awareness and freedom to love generously and outwardly.

Sense of place is therefore both centrifugal *and* centripetal, outward and inward oriented. While places serve as an *axis mundi*, they must also be oriented outward toward the world. Rod Dreher's so-called Benedict Option, for example, which sees monasticism as a model of circling the wagons to save Christian civilization from the secular barbarian hordes, comes across as exclusivist, elitist, and bigoted.[129] An authentic sense of place should be porous to the world without being identical with it.

Even Wendell Berry, accused of romanticization, admits that places are not isolated strongholds of cultural holdout but a network of human settlements that make their living within the limits of the biosphere as a whole. In *Sex, Economy, Freedom, and Community* (1993), he writes, "We are connected by work even to the places where we don't work, for all places are connected; it is clear by now that we cannot exempt one place from our ruin of another."[130] Far from a parochial insularity, Berry elevates the *primacy* of place but not its supremacy, and certainly not at the expense of a global justice-oriented sensibility.

Monks are also unlikely to reify nature into a separate domain of reality, like the preservationists criticized by Plumwood and Bauman. Catholic monks do not hold to any misanthropic notions, sometimes alluded to in deep ecology circles, that the land would be better off without us. Theirs is an anthropocosmic (rather than anthropocentric) ethic that embeds human beings in a theocentric sacred cosmos.[131] The monastic vocation of stewardship is one of cooperation with God in making a place beautiful and inhabitable for the whole of creation. Making a living has meant modifying the land, and a responsible monastic community tries to harmonize their need to live with the ecological community of the surrounding landscape. The monastic communities in this study are in no way perfect in this execution and have much to learn from conservationists, sustainability experts, and the many orders of sisters and nuns who have integrated creation-care more deeply into their liturgies and ways of life.[132]

With respect to the analogy of monogamy versus polygamy, monastics exhibit a kind of liminal position between the two. Monks are celibate individuals living together in community. Monastics could, however, also be said to be "married" to a community and even to the land. This could arguably be a species of spiritual polyamory, though I am sure the monks would balk at this characterization. Regardless, "marriage" would only be a temporary placeholder for the love that binds them to one another, to the land, and to God.

Furthermore, Plumwood and Bauman have suggested that sense of place is more about a romantic sense of nature or an attempt to recover a nostalgic past that ignores global socioecological realities. However, there is nothing particularly naïve or simplistic about the day-in and day-out commitment to a place that is mirrored in many successful monogamous relationships. Commitment to a person or place requires work, vigilance, and dedication and can sometimes be frustrating, heartbreaking, and painful. It is perhaps polyamory, with its imagined freedom to move between any number of relationships with varying levels of intimacy in the pursuit of fulfilling any number of personal desires, that seems ethically problematic considering the greater impact global crises are having on actual places. The commitment to a single community and a single place is precisely what gives one the energy, resolve, and perseverance to face the darker realities of self and other, rather than drifting from place to place as an experience-hungry pilgrim.

As the world's places face uncertain futures, it is not romanticism that monastics teach us but wholehearted devotion. For example, New Camaldoli Hermitage has struggled through many seasons of wildfires and landslides. During winter of 2016–17 the hermitage received record amounts of rains, resulting in mudslides that closed Pacific Coast Highway 1 at two locations, one north and the other just south of the hermitage. These mudslides cut off the community from the wider world for weeks. In addition, the rains have caused several hundred thousand dollars' worth of damage to the hermitage's driveway, which remained practically impassable for several months. Because the hermitage relies on retreatants as a main source of income, this forced isolation has caused significant hardship to the monastery, forcing them to ration food and raise funds from outside to stay afloat. In my correspondence with the monks, however, they remained optimistic and honored by the outpouring of support. They also remained resolutely committed to their hermitage perched above the Pacific Ocean, despite the difficulties, hardship, and uncertainty of what climate change is doing to the place.

Our Lady of Guadalupe Abbey committed to their place even after they realized it had been deforested by the previous landowner. Since the 1950s, they have reforested 880 acres and maintain an ecologically sustainable forestry operation.

Christ in the Desert Abbey has painstakingly sought to improve the sandy desert soil's health through the application of natural fertilizers over many years as they prepare to take on more agricultural work in line with their vision of Benedictine monasticism. The location may not be ideal for farming, but they are committed to making a living there and to embodying the vocation of monks who, as much as they can, live by their own labor.

Two Visions of Place in the Anthropocene

As we approach this brave new world industrial humans are creating, the environmental movement, charged with protecting our common home, is divided. Calls for expanding protected areas are being met with calls to abolish the idea of wilderness altogether. Calls to simplify our technology are being met with calls to intensify it. These ongoing moral conversations (*conversatio morum*) will determine how we proceed in the Anthropocene and whether we perceive it as a threat or a promise. With respect to place, at least two very different views are emerging within the wider environmental movement.

For some environmentalists, despite many obstacles and challenges yet to be overcome, the idea of the Anthropocene inspires great promise. A host of self-styled "ecopragmatists," "ecomodernists," and "new environmentalists" are suggesting that we might foresee the day when our understanding of the planet as a complex system will enable us to fully manage its cycles of weather, climate, and ecosystem services.

In the 2015 *Ecomodernist Manifesto*, more than a dozen authors align themselves with the view that nuclear energy is critical to solving the ecological crisis, that genetic engineering of crops and

intensification of cities will enable a recovery of wild nature, and that
the human population will peak and then decline on its own. The
authors are confident that through the continued advance of science
and technology, we can engineer a planet where both humans and
nonhumans alike can flourish. They are confident that the Anthropocene will be a step forward, not backward. "As scholars, scientists,
campaigners, and citizens," they contend, "we write with the convic-
tion that knowledge and technology, applied with wisdom, might
allow for a good, or even great, Anthropocene. A good Anthropocene demands that humans use their growing social, economic, and
technological powers to make life better for people, stabilize the
climate, and protect the natural world."[133] Even in a warmer world,
human ingenuity will save us, and we can expect, with the proper
adjustments to institutions, economies, and technologies, a Tony the
Tiger–style "grrrrreat!" Anthropocene.

These Anthropocene boosters have more confidence in human
genius than in the human heart, and for many, solving the ecological
crisis is less a moral imperative than it is a technological opportunity.
Human beings have reached the status of gods who have substantial
control over the earth and its myriad life-forms.[134] The value of the
earth community does not exist in its own right; it only reflects what
we value.

The impact to place attachment and sense of place in this vision
would be considerable. One of their great hopes is that human beings might "decouple" ourselves from a reliance on large swaths of
global ecosystems. Decoupling means untangling ourselves from
reliance on a given product such as wood. For example, in Haiti,
trees are often cut down to make charcoal for cooking. If Haitians
were merely provided with a cheaper alternative, they would stop
cutting down so many trees, solving the problem of deforestation.
The less we rely on commodities that alter sensitive ecosystems, the
less impact we are likely to have, especially with a global population likely to exceed ten billion by 2100. The manifesto proclaims:
"Human technologies, from those that first enabled agriculture to
replace hunting and gathering, to those that drive today's globalized

economy, have made humans less reliant upon the many ecosystems that once provided their only sustenance, even as those same ecosystems have often been left deeply damaged."[135] Rural and premodern livelihoods, they argue, have historically supported a lower standard of living and exerted a greater impact on local ecosystems. Ecomodernists are confident that more and better technology will enable us to leave vast tracts of land to recover naturally as we crowd into dense techno-cities fueled by next-generation nuclear, thorium, and hydrogen plants.

Though the authors claim to be writing their manifesto "out of a deep love and emotional connection to the natural world," their vision of a technologically advanced and primarily urban global civilization contradicts and even seems to threaten many Indigenous and rural ways of life that are rooted in and attached to their places.

~ : ~

The other wing of the Anthropocene spectrum sees a bioregional, place-based lifestyle as our best option for weathering the storm ahead. One writer who is horrified by the ecomodernist vision and sees the Anthropocene as a threat rather than a promise is British novelist, essayist, and self-professed "recovering environmentalist" Paul Kingsnorth. For Kingsnorth, the mainstream environmental movement has been co-opted by ecomodernist tendencies to convert the earth into a human-centered techno-paradise. For Kingsnorth, much of what constitutes contemporary environmentalism has simply traded one technological solution for another: "Now it seemed that environmentalism was not about wildness or ecocentrism or the other-than-human world and our relationship to it. Instead, it was about (human) social justice and (human) equality and (human) progress and ensuring that all these things could be realized without degrading the (human) resource base that we used to call nature back when we were being naïve and problematic."[136] As long as environmentalism is an ally in the project of saving the modern industrial way of life, Kingsnorth argues, it has admitted defeat. As a civilization, we are passing through a collective dark night of the

soul, and Kingsnorth wants us to come to grips with the real pos-
sibility and, for him, inevitability of a global civilizational collapse.

For Kingsnorth, environmentalism has made a deal with the devil
and in the process lost its soul. In pursuit of an earthly paradise, environmentalists are unwittingly participating in creating a hell on
earth. Kingsnorth advocates withdrawal from the world under the
assumption that it cannot in fact be evangelized or changed without
fundamentally jeopardizing one's ability to live an authentic human
life. For Kingsnorth, dwelling in and forging relationship to place is
not, however, an escape from the world but rather an essential component of what it means to live in the world in the first place.

His place-based vision calls on artists and others to regroup,
gather in small communities, and begin to truly live again. His former project, the Dark Mountain (which published an "Uncivilized"
manifesto of its own), seeks to reimagine the stories of our place in
the wider earth community and our kinship with particular places.

Rather than insisting on a constant string of actions and reac-
tions, Kingsnorth has personally decided to give up on mainstream
environmental activism. He has opted for a kind of contemplation
as action to focus himself on developing a deep emotional and spiritual connection with actual organisms and in an actual place. Having spent many years as a frontline activist, he decided to pour his
energy into his relationship to a two-and-a-half-acre property in the
countryside of Ireland, where he recently relocated with his small
family. To his critics, Kingsnorth quotes artist Ian Hamilton Finlay,
who was also accused of escapism when he moved to a rural property: "Certain gardens are described as retreats when they are really
attacks.... You can change a bit of the actual world by taking out a
spade."[137]

Though I don't always agree with Kingsnorth's reactionary op-
position to environmentalism, technology, or what he calls "the machine," I cannot help but notice echoes of a kind of monastic spiritual ecology in his trajectory. In fact, as I recently learned, during
the first waves of the Covid-19 pandemic quarantines, Kingsnorth
converted to Eastern Orthodox Christianity, so I was not far off.

Monks see themselves not as running away from the world but as running toward God. Saint Benedict himself left Rome in disgust and founded his monasteries as self-sufficient communities during the long, slow collapse of the Roman Empire. Monasticism insists on first living a life of authenticity. Technology, money, and economic progress are all placed in *right order*, as the monks might say of their overarching values. Kingsnorth, in controversially refusing to play the carbon game or join the chorus of renewable-energy boosters, taps into this insistence that our lives are not about ourselves, that maintaining a standard of living which is both materially and spiritually unsustainable is ultimately a fool's errand.

His disdain for technology was often shared by the monks I met, who, while not professed primitivists, nevertheless remained wary of technology's uses and scope within their communities. The monks have restricted access to the internet, generally do not use cell phones, and seldom watch television. They are critical of overconsumption, pollution, and the excessive use of pesticides (though some communities use it out of necessity).

The monks of Our Lady of Guadalupe and Christ in the Desert refuse to use genetically modified seeds in their gardens. Certainly, there are ongoing debates within the monastic communities regarding technology, from the use of leaf blowers to the availability of personal computers or cell phones, or the monks' presence on some social media accounts to draw in new vocations. But monastic communities strive to balance the needs of the community with the contemplative life they have all committed to living.

To the extent that human institutions rally to the pursuit of a fleeting human progress or technological solutions to moral problems, contemplatives and monastics alike will remain skeptical. Ecomodernists continue to advocate for technology-based solutions to ecological problems that overlook the importance of already deeply forged relationships to place and the land. Human values are the only values that matter in decision-making, and they aspire to shape the earth in our image. On the other hand, postenvironmentalists like Paul Kingsnorth are trying to break the spell of the technological treadmill and sink deep roots into place, even if that means weathering the eventual transformation of the global system as we know it, much as Benedictine monasticism did through the long collapse of the Roman Empire.

Crucially, I am not arguing that monasticism is a model that should be *scaled up* and spread around the world. Rather, I hope what I have shown is that monasticism is a model of how each of us might learn to *scale down*, sink roots into our places, and begin to listen to and learn from them—to care for them as fellow beings, not as engineers.

Epilogue

To know these things, I must ask the place.

WENDELL BERRY

I usually hear the ravens before I see them—a deep, guttural gargle or bark. Ravens are less common in the city and typically live in smaller groups along the rocky coasts of my home in the province of British Columbia. There are, of course, lots of crows in Vancouver. In fact, every night before the vesper dusk, thousands of them rush from all over the Lower Mainland toward their roosts in a certain Burnaby neighborhood. It is like a river of the night has come to life and shattered into a thousand raucous pieces.

In spring 2020, as the Covid-19 pandemic lockdowns raged, the cherry blossoms dared us to despair. My teaching had gone online, and I wasn't seeing anyone in person except for a few close friends. I would go on long walks in Mountainview Cemetery or Queen Elizabeth Park, places closer to home than the north shore provincial parks I was accustomed to driving to for hikes in the forest.

During one of my daily walks, I noticed that a family of ravens had moved into the park. The local crows were none too happy about it, but to me it was something of a grace. I would stop to watch the family of ravens gather materials for their nest and nervously hover about their baby as she learned to forage and fly.

Raven is a sacred being to most Coast Salish and many other Indigenous peoples of the Pacific Northwest. He is a creator-being and trickster-like figure who brought the sun out of a cedar box jealously guarded by an ancient chief. Ravens also appear in Norse stories as the messengers and spies of Odin, and in Greek mythology they were bad omens associated with Apollo's gift of prophecy. It was a raven that, in the Bible, brought the prophet Elijah bread in the wilderness.

Queen Elizabeth Park is a high place in Vancouver, its height the remnant of a basalt intrusion to the more ephemeral till and sands that make up the soils of Vancouver. Before settlers came, it was an old-growth forest, and perhaps even the spawning ground for a run of salmon. It became the site of a quarry, its bones wrested from the hill to build the buildings and mansions of a young, industrializing city. In the 1930s efforts began to convert the spent quarry into a garden. From Indigenous place, to industrial waste, to garden.

Today the park has a rose garden, lawn bowling, a tropical conservatory that houses rare birds, a minigolf course, event venues, a fountain, and several recreational sporting courts. The park also boasts dozens of local and exotic tree and plant species, including giant sequoia and California redwood. These towering trees always remind me of my home state and my time at New Camaldoli Hermitage.

During the pandemic lockdowns and since, I have spent many hours walking among the trees of Queen Elizabeth Park. It is not an intact rainforest like Pacific Spirit Park at the University of British Columbia or the extensive regional and provincial parks that British Columbia is famous for, but it is close to home, and when I have time I go there. It has become a sacred place for me, a chapel for celebrating the liturgy of place and watching the wax and wane of the passing seasons as they silently fade into memory. But Vancouver evokes more than one feeling in me. And I confess that Vancouver is a complicated place for me to belong to.

In monastic and Catholic spirituality more generally, an examination of conscience is a reflection on one's actions or the day's happenings. How did I treat people? What were my thoughts focused on? What occupied my time? Did I lose my temper? Was I kind? Did I remember to be grateful? A robust sense of place must include something like an ecological examination of conscience.

One of the tensions I feel living in Vancouver is that it is a lonely place. It has an international reputation for its natural beauty and commitment to environmental sustainability. In fact, it has set a goal to become the greenest city in the world. Yet what does it say that the so-called greenest city is also known as one of the loneliest cities in North America?[138]

I have lived in Vancouver for a decade at the time of this writing, and my sense of place has deepened since my fieldwork-pilgrimage. I have made some wonderful connections and friends, but it is hard to say I have built anything like a community. It is hard to build a sense of place by myself, and as much as I love the parks and forests, I sometimes wonder if I would be more successful at feeling part of the wider community somewhere else.

Vancouver is also a contested place. It is located within the traditional homeplaces of the Musqueam people, parts of which have also been inhabited and loved by the Tsleil-Waututh and Squamish peoples, by their own reckoning, from time immemorial. For Indigenous peoples of British Columbia, reclaiming access, rights, title, or comanagement of their places is an act of historical justice and healing from cultural trauma.

Many of us living in North America are of settler-colonial ancestry—those who came from Europe as invaders, traders, refugees, slaves, servants, pilgrims. Others came as immigrants from all over the world seeking a better opportunity and a better life. Many of us are trying to come to terms with the fact that we live in places that have been stewarded and loved for thousands of years by Indigenous peoples, some of which were never ceded through treaties. An important dimension of my own conflicted sense of place is acknowledging and honoring the Indigenous peoples whose territories I now dwell on, wrestling with that reality and opening myself to whatever may need to come next.

This can be a contentious conversation for some. However, it is important for settlers to remember that the privileges that come with our ancestry are not an original sin but a call to serve. Honoring the Indigenous heritage of our places is not simply paying deference to the latest politically correct talking points; acknowledging Indigenous peoples is an act of collective penance, responsibility, and reconciliation.

In addition, I must admit to myself that I will never belong to this place in the same way that Indigenous peoples do. But belonging is worth striving for, even in such a messy political ecology. I continue to wrestle with the fact that my ancestral culture's settlement here was an ecclesial-imperial project fueled by a European refugee crisis that spilled over the Atlantic starting some five hundred years ago.

In attending to a liturgy of place, it is not enough to simply spend more time outside or even to learn about the science of our local ecologies. The difficult history of colonization is an important dimension of reckoning with place. Sense of place needs to get comfortable with the discomfort of these past injustices.

My sense of place must include an awareness that the rocky beaches where I roam, the forest parks where I hike, and the mountains I climb are not simply oases of a primordial wild nature but places that called forth their first human caretakers during mythical time, peoples who, starting in the nineteenth century, have been systematically marginalized or dispossessed from the places that gifted them their names in a time beyond time.

My deep spiritual connection to trees must not ignore the scars of that attempted cultural erasure which persists in the moldering cinnamon-red stumps of massive western red cedar trees, whose boles were harvested by opportunistic settlers, many of whom shared my pigmentation. There are no easy arrivals at peace of mind for me. A liturgy of place, like the Psalms of lament, must encompass the beauty *and* the pain of life.

I take comfort in something that Robin Wall Kimmerer writes in *Braiding Sweetgrass*. She teaches the reader how to care for plants and how plants care for us. In one chapter she talks about the idea of "invasive" plants as a symbol of imperial humans. For Kimmerer, not all recent arrivals are alien species that need to be eradicated. Plantain, for example, tagged along with European settlers to North America. The plant, which has an abundance of medicinal uses, has found a place among its native floral companions rather than pushing them out as some nonnative species do (at least initially). Plantain has learned to be a good neighbor and partner to the world as it was found; it did not attempt to remake the world in its own image. Would that my ancestors could have modeled such protocols as we poured over the Atlantic Ocean from Europe, that they could have listened and learned from the caretakers of this land rather than infect them, marginalize them, attempt to convert them, and murder them.

In addition to responding to climate change's impacts on our places, those of us of settler and immigrant backgrounds must engage in the hard work of becoming good neighbors in our places, doing what we can to make historical injustices right. Whether our ancestors were created here, settled here many generations ago, or recently arrived as refugees from Syria or Ukraine, belonging to a place means listening to the place and striving to become a better neighbor.

No matter where you live, there are manifold ways to forge deeper connections with your places. Here are a few suggestions from my own ongoing, evolving, and sometimes tortured practice of place-making:

- Learn the Indigenous history and place-names of your place.

- If you live in North America, support organizations that are seeking to reclaim territory for Indigenous peoples or work with survivors of colonial residential or boarding school systems.

- Learn the history of the waves of settlement or colonization in your place, especially in areas that might be considered natural or wild.

- Learn about your own ancestry and cultural heritage and the places your people came from.

- Locate and visit the graves of your immediate ancestors. If you can, visit them on the anniversaries of their death or on All Souls' Day.

- Commit to a regular practice of contemplative walking, even in the city.

- If you are Christian, consider praying the Liturgy of the Hours. If you are not, collect a small notebook of cherished poetry and try reading it regularly during the hinges of the day (dawn and dusk).

+ If you live near one, visit a regional or local protected area regularly. Support efforts to restore lands to ecological health.

+ Craft a ritual for honoring the seasons, the equinoxes, and the solstices.

+ Become aware of the phases of the moon. Mark the new and full moons with some intentional act or ritual.

+ Track the cycle of a planet you feel akin to and try to observe its cycles in the sky.

+ Make a chart with the seasonal harvest times for native fruits, berries, and mushrooms.

+ Learn the common, Latin, and/or Indigenous names for native and medicinal plants that grow in your area.

+ Identify local birding organizations and learn the permanent and migratory birds that inhabit your region.

+ Take a course or download an app that identifies birdsong so you can begin to understand your local soundscape.

+ Learn the contours and tributaries of your micro and macro watersheds.

+ Support local artists, farmers, gardeners, herbalists, artisans, businesses, and nonprofit organizations.

+ Be attentive to changes in your homeplace, even the ones you don't like.

+ Spend time in a damaged or degraded place like a clear-cut forest and try to stay with the discomfort that comes up there. Seek out small examples of beauty or leave some kind of visual offering to the place that represents your sorrow or hope for healing.

+ Keep a journal of your wanderings, memories, and feelings while you are out on the land.

+ Gather with others on the land. Talk, tell stories, organize for change.

+ Try to connect the ways your habits and purchased products impact people and the land in your community and places around the world.

+ If you are able, grow a garden. Or, if you live in an apartment, try potted plants.

ACKNOWLEDGMENTS

I would like to acknowledge and thank the places I have called home. First, the place that called me into being, Orange County, California; the place I called home until the age of twenty-one, the traditional territory of the Tongva, Chumash, Acjachemen, and Payómkawichum peoples who have stewarded this place from time immemorial. What a strange and beautiful place you are. Thank you for your abundance and your lessons.

I would like to acknowledge and thank the Dominican Republic, where I spent two years as an LDS missionary; the ancestral home of the Taino peoples. The population suffered disease, exploitation, and genocide at the hands of colonists, but their spirit lives on in the Dominican people. Thank you for your lush beauty.

I would like to acknowledge and thank Utah, where I lived as an undergraduate and for two years after graduate school; the territory of the Ute, Paiute, Dine, Goshute, and Shoshone peoples who stewarded this place from time immemorial. The place of my ancestors on my mother's side. My Mormon heritage. Thank you for welcoming me back and keeping the memory of belonging.

I would like to acknowledge New Haven, Connecticut, where I lived for three years for graduate school; traditional territory of the Quinnipiac (Eansketambawg) people who have stewarded this place from time immemorial. I knew you only briefly, but I thank you for nurturing me during times of crisis and transition.

Finally, I would like to acknowledge and thank Vancouver, British Columbia, where I have lived since 2013; traditional and unceded territories of the Musqueam Tsleil-Waututh and Squamish peoples.

You are a beautiful spiritual ecology of mountain, ocean, and forest. Thank you for nourishing my restless heart.

I would also like to acknowledge the people who made writing this book possible. I want to thank my doctoral supervisor, Terre Satterfield, for her support, mentorship, and friendship. Her presence in my life was one of the highlights of my career as a student. I want to thank mentor and friend Mike Meitner for serving on my committee and their UBC courses. Also, many thanks to Susan Power Bratton for her encouragement and for believing in this book. Many thanks to the support staff at the Institute for Resources Environment and Sustainability, Gillian Harris, Linda Stewart, Stefanie Ickert, Lisa Johannesen, and Bonnie Leung. I want to thank my family, J, Holli, Ashli, Jacob, Jordan, Brad, Sarah, Claire, Drew, Eleanor, and John, for their love and support. I want to also thank Rachael and Maya for their companionship during different legs of this journey. I want to thank Trinity University Press, and especially my editor, Steffanie Mortis Stevens. Her keen eye has helped me craft my dissertation into a readable story. I want to thank Rudiger Krause, Paul Rowe, and Eric Mason for their willingness to read drafts of this manuscript, and Jillian Froebe for providing a sanctuary to work on the final revisions.

Finally, I want to acknowledge the monks in this book and the lands they keep. I could not have written this book without the monks who humored me and walked with me and talked with me at the communities of New Camaldoli Hermitage, New Clairvaux Abbey, Our Lady of Guadalupe Abbey, and Christ in the Desert. I want to thank Abbot Peter, Abbot Mark, Prior Cyprian, and Father Benedict for believing this to be a worthwhile pursuit and opening their communities to me.

~: :~

All excerpts from the Psalms are taken from the Benedictine Monks of Conception Abbey, *The Revised Grail Psalms: A Liturgical Psalter* (Collegeville: Liturgical Press, 2010).

Some of the wording and all the data from this book comes from my doctoral dissertation, "Dwelling in the Wilderness: Place, Landscape, and the Sacred among Catholic Monks of the American West" (PhD diss., University of British Columbia, 2017).

Several topics and content from the chapters also appear in my articles "The 'Greening' of Christian Monasticism and the Future of Monastic Landscapes in North America," *Religions* 10, no. 7 (2019); and "Charged Moments: Landscape and the Experience of the Sacred among Catholic Monks in North America," *Religions* 10, no. 2 (2019).

I also discuss monastic forestry in my article "Managing for Ecological and Spiritual Values: A Brief History of Monastic Forestry," *Forest History Today* 27, nos. 1–2 (Spring/Fall 2022): 22–31.

The section titled "Wrestling with God on the Rio Chama" is based on a blog post I wrote in 2016 at https://holyscapes.org/2016/04/23/wrestling-with-god-on-the-chama-river.

Several ideas and phrasings in "Monastic Wisdom for the Anthropocene" appeared in my 2018 essay "In the Presence of Absence: A Spiritual Ecology of the Transcendent" at https://holyscapes.org/2018/09/10/in-the-presence-of-absence-a-spiritual-ecology-of-the-transcendent.

NOTES

Introduction

1. Thomas Merton, *The Wisdom of the Desert: Sayings from the Desert Fathers of the Fourth Century* (New York: New Directions, 1960), 4.

2. This interdisciplinary field helps me connect religious studies, philosophy, forestry, anthropology, and theology. Some refer to it as environmental humanities. My actual doctoral degree was issued in resources, environment, and sustainability.

3. John Wylie, *Landscape* (New York: Routledge, 2007).

4. Yi-Fu Tuan, *Topophilia: A Study of Environmental Perceptions, Attitudes, and Values* (New York: Columbia University Press, [1974] 1990), 112.

5. Maria Lewicka, "Place Attachment: How Far Have We Come in the Last Forty Years?," *Journal of Environmental Psychology* 31, no. 3 (August 31, 2011): 207–30.

6. Jeff Malpas, *Place and Experience: A Philosophical Topography* (New York: Routledge, 2018).

7. Paul J. Crutzen, "The Anthropocene," in *Earth System Science in the Anthropocene: Emerging Issues and Problems*, ed. Eckhart Ehlers and Thomas Krafft, 13–18 (Berlin: Springer, 2006).

8. Will Steffen, Jacques Grinevald, Paul Crutzen, and John McNeill, "The Anthropocene: Conceptual and Historical Perspectives," *Philosophical Transactions of the Royal Society A* 369, no. 1938 (March 12, 2011): 842–67.

9. Elizabeth Kolbert, *The Sixth Extinction: An Unnatural History* (New York: Henry Holt, 2014).

10. Mika Rantanen et al., "The Arctic Has Warmed Nearly Four Times Faster Than the Globe Since 1979," *Communications Earth and Environment* 3, no. 1 (2022): 168.

11. Hans Otto Pörtner et al., *IPCC, 2022: Climate Change 2022: Impacts, Adaptation, and Vulnerability. Contribution of Working Group II to the Sixth Assessment Report of the Intergovernmental Panel on Climate* (New York: Cambridge University Press, 2022).

12. Pope Francis, *Laudato Si': Care for Our Common Home* (Vatican City: Vatican Press, 2015).

13. Kyle Whyte, "Our Ancestors' Dystopia Now," in *Routledge Companion to the Environmental Humanities*, ed. Ursula Heise, Jon Christensen, and Michelle Niemann, 206–16 (New York: Routledge, 2017).

14. Aldo Leopold, *A Sand County Almanac: With Other Essays on Conservation from Round River* (New York: Oxford University Press, [1949] 1968), viii.

15. John Gatta, *Making Nature Sacred: Literature, Religion, and Environment in America from the Puritans to the Present* (New York: Oxford University Press, 2004), 18.

16. Henry David Thoreau, *Walking* (Digireads.com, [1851] 2011), 455/763.

17. Thoreau, *Walking*, 514/763.

18. Thoreau, *Walking*, 508/763.

19. *The National Parks: America's Best Idea* (PBS, 2009).

20. William Cronon, "The Trouble with Wilderness; or, Getting Back to the Wrong Nature," in *Uncommon Ground: Rethinking the Human Place in Nature*, ed. William Cronon, 80 (New York: W. W. Norton, 1995).

21. Tim Ingold, *The Perception of the Environment: Essays on Livelihood, Dwelling, and Skill* (New York: Routledge, 2000).

22. Lynn White Jr., "The Historical Roots of Our Ecological Crisis," *Science* 155, no. 3767 (1967), 1203–7.

23. Paul Kingsnorth, "Introduction," in *The World-Ending Fire: The Essential Wendell Berry*, ed. Paul Kingsnorth, x (Berkeley: Counterpoint, 2017).

24. Saint Athanasius, *Life of Anthony*, vol. 4 of *Nicene and Post-Nicene Fathers*, ed. Philip Schaff and Henry Wace (Buffalo: Christian Literature Publishing, 1894), 50.

25. William P. Brown, *Seeing the Psalms: A Theology of Metaphor* (Westminster: John Knox Press, 2002).

26. Hermann Gunkel, *An Introduction to the Psalms* (Macon: Mercer University Press, [1933] 1998).

27. Flannery O'Connor, *The Habit of Being: Letters of Flannery O'Connor* (New York: Farrar, Straus and Giroux, 1988), 55.

28. J. P. Williams, *Seeking the God Beyond: A Beginner's Guide to Christian Apophatic Spirituality* (Eugene: Cascade Books, 2019).

29. Michael Casey, *Lectio Divina: The Ancient Art of Lectio Divina* (Chicago: Triumph Books, 1996).

30. Llewellyn Vaughn-Lee, *Spiritual Ecology: The Cry of the Earth* (Point Reyes: Golden Sufi Center, 2013), v.

31. Kathleen Norris, *The Cloister Walk* (New York: Penguin, 1996).

32. Douglas E. Christie, *The Blue Sapphire of the Mind: Notes for a Contemplative Ecology* (New York: Oxford University Press, 2013).

33. Sarah McFarland Taylor, *Green Sisters: A Spiritual Ecology* (Cambridge, Mass.: Harvard University Press, 2007), 20.

34. While those killed for their beliefs were called red martyrs, after the persecution ceased, those who sacrificed the comforts of society were called white martyrs.

35. Belden Lane, *The Solace of Fierce Landscapes: Exploring Desert and Mountain Spirituality* (New York: Oxford University Press, 198), 37.

36. Susan P. Bratton, *Christianity, Wilderness, and Wildlife: The Original Desert Solitaire* (Scranton: University of Scranton Press, 1993), 165–69.

37. Robert Hale, *Love on the Mountain: The Chronicle Journal of a Camaldolese Monk* (Naperville: Source Books, 1999), 34.

38. Kat Anderson, *Tending the Wild: Native American Knowledge and the Management of California's Natural Resources* (Berkeley: University of California Press, 2013).

39. Gary S. Breschini and Trudy Haversat, "An Overview of the Esselen Indians of Monterey County" (2001), www.bigsurcalifornia.org/esselen.html.

40. California State Parks, *Limekiln State Park* (Big Sur: California State Parks, 1998).

41. Bruno Barnhart, *The Second Simplicity* (Mahwah: Paulist Press, 1999); *The Future of Wisdom: Toward a Rebirth of Sapiential Christianity* (New York: Continuum, 2007).

42. Timothy Fry, OSB, ed., *RB 1980: The Rule of Saint Benedict in English* (Collegeville: Liturgical Press, 1982), 15. According to the Rule of Saint Benedict, sarabaites are another type of monk after gyrovagues, cenobites, and hermits. They lived in one place but refused to live by a rule or under a superior.

43. Stephen Harding, "Exordium Parvum," Order of Cistercians of the Strict Observance, www.ocso.org/resources/foundational-text/exordium-parvum (accessed March 1, 2023).

44. Daniel Hillel, *The Natural History of the Bible: An Environmental Exploration of the Hebrew Scriptures* (New York: Columbia University Press, 2006).

45. Walter Brueggemann, *Land* (Minneapolis: Fortress Press, 2002), 312–13/3422.

46. Terrance Deacon, *The Symbolic Species: The Co-evolution of Language and the Brain* (New York: W. W. Norton, 1997).

47. Denis Cosgrove and Stephen Daniels, *The Iconography of Landscape: Essays on the Symbolic Representation, Design, and Use of Past Environments* (New York: Cambridge University Press, 1988), 1.

48. Simon Schama, *Landscape and Memory* (Toronto: Random House, 1995), 61.

49. Michel de Certeau, *The Practice of Everyday Life* (Berkeley: University of California Press, [1984] 2011), 43.

50. G. K. Anderson, "Designed for Prayer: A Bibliographical Essay on Medieval Monasticism for Contemporary Designers and Gardeners," *Cistercian Studies Quarterly* 36, no. 4 (2001): 457.

51. See *Aeneid*, book 6, lines 619–55, cited in Jean Delumeau, *History of Paradise: The Garden of Eden in Myth and Tradition* (New York: Continuum, 1995), 8.

52. "The mountains melt like wax / before the face of the Lord" (Psalm 97).

53. Yi-Fu Tuan, *Topophilia*, 112.

54. Maurice Merleau-Ponty, *Phenomenology of Perception* (New York: Routledge, [1962] 2002), 249.

55. Richard Nelson, *The Island Within* (New York: Vintage, 1989), 249.

56. James J. Gibson, *The Ecological Approach to Visual Perception* (Hillsdale: Lawrence Erlbaum, 1986).

57. David Abram, *Spell of the Sensuous: Perception and Language in a More-Than-Human World* (New York: Vintage Books, 1996), 68.

58. Keith Basso, *Wisdom Sits in Places: Landscape and Language among the Western Apache* (Albuquerque: University of New Mexico Press, 1996).

To Blossom as the Rose

59. Ellen F. Arnold, *Negotiating the Landscape: Environment and Monastic Identity in the Medieval Ardennes* (Philadelphia: University of Pennsylvania Press, 2013), 7.

60. Pierre Riché, *The Carolingians: A Family Who Forged Europe* (Philadelphia: University of Pennsylvania Press, 1993), 22.

61. Cited in Janet E. Burton and Julie Kerr, *The Cistercians in the Middle Ages* (Suffolk: Boydell Press, 2011), 12.

62. Burton and Kerr, *Cistercians*, 16.

63. David D. Perata, *The Orchards of Perseverance: Conversations with Trappist Monks about God, Their Lives, and the World* (Ruthven, Iowa: St. Therese's Press, 2000), 9.

64. Terrance Kardong, "Monks and the Land," *Cistercian Studies Quarterly* 18, no. 2 (1983): 135–48.

65. Romano Guardini, *The Spirit of the Liturgy* (San Francisco: Ignatius Press, [1930] 2018), 36.

66. "Liturgy of the Hours," USCCB, www.usccb.org/prayer-and-worship /liturgy-of-the-hours (accessed March 1, 2023).

67. Edward Casey, *Getting Back into Place* (Bloomington: Indiana University Press, 1993), 21.

68. Pierre Bourdieu, *The Logic of Practice* (Queensland: Polity Press, 1990).

69. Christopher Brooke, *The Age of the Cloister: The Story of Monastic Life in the Middle Ages* (Mahwah: Paulist Press, 2003), 75.

70. Casey, *Getting Back into Place*, 32.

71. Stephen Jenkinson, *Die Wise* (Berkeley: North Atlantic Books, 2015), 252.

72. Thomas Merton, *Conjectures of a Guilty Bystander* (New York: Image Books, [1968] 2009), 141–42.

Seeing the Forest and the Trees

73. Martinus Cawley, *Monks of Jordan, 1904–2004* (Lafayette: Guadalupe Translations, 2004); Martinus Cawley, *Guadalupe's Pecos Years: History of Our Lady of Guadalupe, Trappist Abbey During the Formative Years at Pecos, New Mexico, 1948–1955* (Lafayette: Guadalupe Translations, 2001).

74. See chapter 48 of Fry, *RB 1980*, 69, my emphasis.

75. Brooke, *Age of the Cloister*, 80.

76. C. H. Lawrence, *Medieval Monasticism: Forms of Religious Life in Western Europe in the Middle Ages* (New York: Routledge, 2001).

77. Michael Casey, "Manual Work in the Rule and Beyond," *Tjurunga*, no. 78 (2010): 39.

78. The original translated quotation is: "Believe me, you will find more lessons in the woods than in books. Trees and stones will teach you what you cannot learn from masters." From Saint Bernard's sermons: epistola CVI, sect. 2, cited in Edward Churton, *The Early English Church* ([1840] 1841), 324.

79. This quotation is attributed to Saint Anthony by Evagrius Ponticus in *Capita Practica ad Anatolium*, cited in Lane, *Solace of Fierce Landscapes*, 165.

80. See Philip H. Pfatteicher, *Liturgical Spirituality* (Valley Forge: Trinity Press, 1997); Joseph Ratzinger, *The Spirit of the Liturgy* (San Francisco: Ignatius Press, [2000] 2018).

81. The actual quotation, translated from the French by Fr. H. Ramière, SJ, is: "Do You not give fecundity to the root hidden underground, and can You not, if You so will, make this darkness in which You are pleased to keep me, fruitful? Live then, little root of my heart, in the deep, invisible heart of God; and by its power, send forth branches, leaves, flowers and fruits, which, although invisible to yourself, are a pure joy and nourishment to others." Jean Pierre de Caussade, *Abandonment to Divine Providence* (Digireads.com, [1861] 2009), 53–54.

82. It appears that Gertrude Stein was referring to the radical changes that had come to pass in her hometown of Oakland, California, since her upbringing there.

83. David Seamon, *A Geography of the Lifeworld: Movement, Rest, and Encounter* (London: Croom Helm, [1979] 2016), 123.

84. This process is also well documented at Mount Angel Abbey in Oregon and Saint Martin's Abbey in Washington. See Neil Yocom, OSB, *Mount of*

Communion: Mount Angel Abbey: 1882–1982 (Mount Angel: Mount Angel Abbey, 1985); John C. Scott, OSB, *This Place Called Saint Martin's, 1895–1995: A Centennial History of Saint Martin's College and Abbey Lacey, Washington* (Virginia Beach: Donning, 1996).

Alone with the Alone

85. Mari Graña, *Brothers of the Desert: The Story of the Monastery of Christ in the Desert* (Santa Fe: Sunstone Press, 2006).

86. Craig Childs, *House of Rain: Tracking a Vanished Civilization across the American Southwest* (Boston: Little, Brown, 2007).

87. Graña, *Brothers of the Desert*, 27.

88. Greg Woolf, "Divinity and Power in Ancient Rome," in *Religion and Power: Divine Kingship in the Ancient World and Beyond*, edited by Nicole Brisch (Chicago: Oriental Institute of the University of Chicago, 2008), 243–61.

89. Yi-Fu Tuan, *Landscapes of Fear* (New York: Pantheon, 2013).

90. John Inge, *A Christian Theology of Place* (New York: Routledge, 2017).

91. Gerard Manley Hopkins, "God's Grandeur," Poetry Foundation, www .poetryfoundation.org/poems/44395/gods-grandeur (accessed March 1, 2023).

92. Thomas Merton, *New Seeds of Contemplation* (New York: New Directions, 1972), 30.

93. Sallie McFague, *The Body of God: An Ecological Theology* (Minneapolis: Fortress Press, 1993), 134. Dr. McFague was a personal mentor of mine.

94. Diana L. Eck, *India: A Sacred Geography* (New York: Harmony, 2011).

95. Eliza F. Kent, *Sacred Groves and Local Gods: Religion and Environmentalism in South India* (New York: Oxford University Press, 2013).

96. Belden Lane, *Landscapes of the Sacred: Geography and Narrative in American Spirituality* (Baltimore: Johns Hopkins University Press, 2001), 19.

97. Lane, *Landscapes of the Sacred*, 19.

98. Pope Francis, *Laudato Si'*, #105, my emphasis.

99. The *hesychia* is the eastern Orthodox Christian tradition of silence; see Christie, *Blue Sapphire of the Mind*, 191.

100. The writer was most likely a sixth-century mystic and monk not alive during the time of Saint Paul, therefore many scholars refer to him as Pseudo-Dionysius. See Dionysius the Areopagite, *On the Divine Names and the Mystical Theology* (Montana: Aeterna Press, 2015), 100.

101. Lane, *Solace of Fierce Landscapes*, 12.

102. Williams, *Seeking the God Beyond*, 79.

103. Pope Francis, *Laudato Si'*, #119.

Monastic Wisdom for the Anthropocene

104. Steffen et al., "The Anthropocene," 842–67.

105. Jason W. Moore, ed., *Anthropocene or Capitalocene? Nature, History, and the Crisis of Capitalism* (Oakland: PM Press, 2016).

106. Nan Shepherd, *The Living Mountain: A Celebration of the Cairngorm Mountains of Scotland* (Edinburgh: Canongate Books, 1977), 40.

107. Robin Wall Kimmerer, *Braiding Sweetgrass: Indigenous Wisdom, Scientific Knowledge, and the Teachings of Plants* (Minneapolis: Milkweed, 2013).

108. Serena Renner, "The Deep Roots of BC's Old Growth Defenders," *The Tyee*, September 16, 2020, https://thetyee.ca/News/2020/09/16/Movement-In-Woods.

109. Cronon, "Trouble with Wilderness," 69–90.

110. Cronon, "Trouble with Wilderness," 69–90.

111. Lane, *Solace of Fierce Landscapes*, 17.

112. Ursula Goodenough, *The Sacred Depths of Nature* (New York: Oxford University Press, 1998).

113. Sara Maitland, *A Book of Silence* (Berkeley: Counterpoint, 2008), 63.

114. Macfarlane, Robert. "The Word-Hoard: Robert Macfarlane on Rewilding Our Language of Landscape," *The Guardian*, Feb. 27, 2015.

115. Glenn Albrecht, "'Solastalgia': A New Concept in Health and Identity," *PAN: Philosophy Activism Nature* 3 (2005): 41–55. See also Glenn Albrecht, *Earth Emotions: New Words for a New World* (Ithaca: Cornell University Press, 2019), 1.

116. Stephen Kellert and E. O. Wilson, *The Biophilia Hypothesis* (New York: Island Press, 1995), 416.

117. Albrecht, *Earth Emotions*, 38.

118. Robert Macfarlane, "Generation Anthropocene: How Humans Have Altered the Planet Forever," *The Guardian*, April 1, 2016.

119. Ashlee Willox Cunsolo et al., "'From This Place and of This Place': Climate Change, Sense of Place, and Health in Nunatsiavut, Canada," *Social Science and Medicine* 75 no. 3 (2012): 538–47.

120. Donna Haraway, *Staying with the Trouble: Making Kin in the Chthulucene* (Durham, NC: Duke University Press, 2016); Thomas Berry, *The Dream of the Earth* (San Francisco: Sierra Club, 1988).

121. Christie, *Blue Sapphire of the Mind*, 121.

122. Trebbe Johnson, *Radical Joy for Hard Times* (Berkeley: North Atlantic Books, 2018).

123. Tamara Hill Murphy, "The Hole in Wendell Berry's Gospel: Why the Agrarian Dream Is Not Enough," *Plough Magazine*, www.plough.com/en/topics/faith/discipleship/the-hole-in-wendell-berrys-gospel (accessed March 1, 2023).

124. Carolyn R. Schaffer and Kristin Anundsen, *Creating Community Anywhere: Finding Support and Connection in a Fragmented World* (New York: G. P. Putnam's Sons, 1993), 6.

125. Lauren Frayer, "Nearly Twenty-Seven Years After Hindu Mob Destroyed a Mosque, the Scars in India Remain Deep," *NPR*, April 25, 2019, www.npr.org /2019/04/25/711412924/nearly-27-years-after-hindu-mob-destroyed-a-mosque -the-scars-in-india-remain-dee.

126. Timothy Morton, *The Ecological Thought* (Cambridge: Harvard University Press, 2010), 8.

127. Val Plumwood, "Shadow Place and the Politics of Dwelling," *Australian Humanities Review* 44 (March 2008): 139–50.

128. Whitney Bauman, *Religion and Ecology: Developing a Planetary Ethic* (New York: Columbia University Press, 2014), 127.

129. Rod Dreher, *The Benedict Option: A Strategy for Christians in a Post-Christian Nation* (New York: Sentinel, 2017).

130. Wendell Berry, *Sex, Economy, Freedom, and Community* (Berkeley: Counterpoint, 1993), 35.

131. Sam Mickey, "Contributions to Anthropocosmic Environmental Ethics," *Worldviews* 11, no. 2 (December 31, 2006): 226–47.

132. Taylor, *Green Sisters*.

133. John L. Asafu-Adjaye et al., *An Ecomodernist Manifesto* (2015), www .ecomodernism.org/manifesto-english (accessed March 1, 2023).

134. Yuval Noah Harari, *Homo Deus: A Brief History of Tomorrow* (London: Harvill Secker, 2015).

135. Asafu-Adjaye et al., *An Ecomodernist Manifesto* (accessed March 1, 2023).

136. Paul Kingsnorth, *Confessions of a Recovering Environmentalist* (Minneapolis: Graywolf Press, 2017), 76.

137. Kingsnorth, *Confessions*, 102–3.

Epilogue

138. Vancouver Foundation, "2012 Connections and Engagement Report," October 19, 2022, www.vancouverfoundation.ca/detail/2012-connections -engagement-report.

SELECTED BIBLIOGRAPHY

Abram, David. *Spell of the Sensuous: Perception and Language in a More-Than-Human World*. New York: Vintage Books, 1996.

Albrecht, Glenn. *Earth Emotions: New Words for a New World*. Ithaca: Cornell University Press, 2019.

Anderson, Kat. *Tending the Wild: Native American Knowledge and the Management of California's Natural Resources*. Berkeley: University of California Press, 2013.

Arnold, Ellen F. *Negotiating the Landscape: Environment and Monastic Identity in the Medieval Ardennes*. Philadelphia: University of Pennsylvania Press, 2013.

Barnhart, Bruno. *The Future of Wisdom: Toward a Rebirth of Sapiential Christianity*. New York: Continuum, 2007.

———. *The Second Simplicity*. Mahwah: Paulist Press, 1999.

Basso, Keith. *Wisdom Sits in Places: Landscape and Language among the Western Apache*. Albuquerque: University of New Mexico Press, 1996.

Bauman, Whitney. *Religion and Ecology: Developing a Planetary Ethic*. New York: Columbia University Press, 2014.

Berry, Thomas. *The Dream of the Earth*. San Francisco: Sierra Club, 1988.

Berry, Wendell. *Sex, Economy, Freedom, and Community*. Berkeley: Counterpoint, 1993.

———. *The World-Ending Fire: The Essential Wendell Berry*. Edited by Paul Kingsnorth. Berkeley: Counterpoint, 2017.

Bratton, Susan P. *Christianity, Wilderness, and Wildlife: The Original Desert Solitaire*. Scranton: University of Scranton Press, 1993.

Brooke, Christopher. *The Age of the Cloister: The Story of Monastic Life in the Middle Ages*. Mahwah: Paulist Press, 2003.

Brown, William P. *Seeing the Psalms: A Theology of Metaphor*. Westminster: John Knox Press, 2002.

Brueggemann, Walter. *Land*. Minneapolis: Fortress Press, 2002.

Burton, Janet E., and Julie Kerr. *The Cistercians in the Middle Ages*. Suffolk: Boydell Press, 2011.

Casey, Edward. *Getting Back into Place*. Bloomington: Indiana University Press, 1993.

Vaughn-Lee, Llewellyn. *Spiritual Ecology: The Cry of the Earth*. Point Reyes: Golden Sufi Center, 2013.

White, Lynn, Jr. "The Historical Roots of Our Ecological Crisis." *Science* 155, no. 3767 (1967): 1203–1207.

Williams, J. P. *Seeking the God Beyond: A Beginner's Guide to Christian Apophatic Spirituality*. Eugene: Cascade Books, 2019.

Wylie, John. *Landscape*. New York: Routledge, 2007.

 Jason M. Brown is a lecturer in the Department of Humanities at Simon Fraser University in British Columbia. He holds a doctoral degree in resources, environment, and sustainability from the University of British Columbia and joint master's degrees from Yale University in forestry and ecology. He lives in Vancouver and blogs at www.holyscapes.org.

Lewicka, Maria. "Place Attachment: How Far Have We Come in the Last Forty Years?" *Journal of Environmental Psychology* 31, no. 3 (August 31, 2011): 207–30.

Maitland, Sara. *A Book of Silence.* Berkeley: Counterpoint, 2008.

McFague, Sallie. *The Body of God: An Ecological Theology.* Minneapolis: Fortress Press, 1993.

Merleau-Ponty, Maurice. *Phenomenology of Perception.* New York: Routledge, [1962] 2002.

Merton, Thomas. *Conjectures of a Guilty Bystander.* New York: Image Books, [1968] 2009.

———. *New Seeds of Contemplation.* New York: New Directions, 1972.

———. *The Wisdom of the Desert: Sayings from the Desert Fathers of the Fourth Century.* New York: New Directions, 1960.

Mickey, Sam. "Contributions to Anthropocosmic Environmental Ethics." *Worldviews* 11, no. 2 (December 31, 2006): 226–47.

Moore, Jason W., ed. *Anthropocene or Capitalocene? Nature, History, and the Crisis of Capitalism.* Oakland: PM Press, 2016.

Morton, Timothy. *The Ecological Thought.* Cambridge, Mass.: Harvard University Press, 2010.

Nelson, Richard. *The Island Within.* New York: Vintage, 1989.

Norris, Kathleen. *The Cloister Walk.* New York: Penguin, 1996.

Perata, David D. *The Orchards of Perseverance: Conversations with Trappist Monks about God, Their Lives, and the World.* Ruthven, Iowa: St. Therese's Press, 2000.

Pfatteicher, Philip H. *Liturgical Spirituality.* Valley Forge: Trinity Press, 1997.

Plumwood, Val. "Shadow Place and the Politics of Dwelling." *Australian Humanities Review*, no. 44 (2008): 139–50.

Ratzinger, Joseph. *The Spirit of the Liturgy.* San Francisco: Ignatius Press, [2000] 2018.

Schama, Simon. *Landscape and Memory.* Toronto: Random House, 1995.

Seamon, David. *A Geography of the Lifeworld: Movement, Rest, and Encounter.* London: Croom Helm, [1979] 2016.

Shepherd, Nan. *The Living Mountain: A Celebration of the Cairngorm Mountains of Scotland.* Edinburgh: Canongate Books, [1977] 2014.

Steffen, Will, Jacques Grinevald, Paul J. Crutzen, and John H. McNeill. "The Anthropocene: Conceptual and Historical Perspectives." *Philosophical Transactions of the Royal Society A* 369, no. 1938 (March 12, 2011): 842–67.

Taylor, Sarah McFarland. *Green Sisters: A Spiritual Ecology.* Cambridge, Mass.: Harvard University Press, 2007.

Tuan, Yi-Fu. *Landscapes of Fear.* New York: Pantheon, 2013.

———. *Topophilia: A Study of Environmental Perceptions, Attitudes, and Values.* New York: Columbia University Press, [1974] 1990.

Casey, Michael, ocso. *Lectio Divina: The Ancient Art of Lectio Divina*. Chicago:
    Triumph Books, 1996.
———. "Manual Work in the Rule and Beyond." *Tjurunga*, no. 78 (2010): 39.
Christie, Douglas E. *The Blue Sapphire of the Mind: Notes for a Contemplative
    Ecology*. New York: Oxford University Press, 2013.
Cronon, William. *Uncommon Ground: Rethinking the Human Place in Nature*. New
    York: W. W. Norton, 1995.
De Certeau, Michel. *The Practice of Everyday Life*. Berkeley: University of
    California Press, [1984] 2011.
Eck, Diana L. *India: A Sacred Geography*. New York: Harmony, 2011.
Francis, Pope. *Laudato Si': Care for Our Common Home*. Vatican City: Vatican
    Press, 2015.
Gibson, James J. *The Ecological Approach to Visual Perception*. Hillsdale: Lawrence
    Erlbaum, 1986.
Graña, Mari. *Brothers of the Desert: The Story of the Monastery of Christ in the
    Desert*. Santa Fe: Sunstone Press, 2006.
Guardini, Romano. *The Spirit of the Liturgy*. San Francisco: Ignatius Press, [1930]
    2018.
Hale, Robert. *Love on the Mountain: The Chronicle Journal of a Camaldolese Monk*.
    Naperville: Source Books, 1999.
Haraway, Donna. *Staying with the Trouble: Making Kin in the Chthulucene*.
    Durham: Duke University Press, 2016.
Hillel, Daniel. *The Natural History of the Bible: An Environmental Exploration of the
    Hebrew Scriptures*. New York: Columbia University Press, 2006.
Inge, John. *A Christian Theology of Place*. New York: Routledge, 2017.
Ingold, Tim. *The Perception of the Environment: Essays on Livelihood, Dwelling, and
    Skill*. New York: Routledge, 2000.
Jenkinson, Stephen. *Die Wise*. Berkeley: North Atlantic Books, 2015.
Johnson, Trebbe. *Radical Joy for Hard Times*. Berkeley: North Atlantic Books, 2018.
Kardong, Terrance. "Monks and the Land." *Cistercian Studies Quarterly* 18, no. 2
    (1983): 135–48.
Kent, Eliza F. *Sacred Groves and Local Gods: Religion and Environmentalism in
    South India*. New York: Oxford University Press, 2013.
Kimmerer, Robin Wall. *Braiding Sweetgrass: Indigenous Wisdom, Scientific
    Knowledge, and the Teachings of Plants*. Minneapolis: Milkweed, 2013.
Lane, Belden. *Landscapes of the Sacred: Geography and Narrative in American
    Spirituality*. Baltimore: Johns Hopkins University Press, 2001.
———. *The Solace of Fierce Landscapes: Exploring Desert and Mountain Spirituality*.
    New York: Oxford, 1998.
Lawrence, C. H. *Medieval Monasticism: Forms of Religious Life in Western Europe in
    the Middle Ages*. New York: Routledge, 2001.